DISCOVERING THE
MAKING OF THE UK

THE SCHOOLS HISTORY PROJECT

This project was set up by the Schools Council in 1972. Its main aim was to suggest suitable objectives for history teachers, and to promote the use of appropriate materials and teaching methods for their realization. This involved a reconsideration of the nature of history and its relevance in secondary schools, the design of a syllabus framework which shows the uses of history in the teaching of adolescents, and the setting up of appropriate examinations.

Since 1978 the project has been based at Trinity and All Saints' College, Leeds. It is now self-funding and with the advent of the National Curriculum it has expanded its publications to provide courses throughout Key Stages 1–3, and for a range of GCSE and A level syllabuses. The project provides INSET for all aspects of National Curriculum, GCSE and A level history, and also publishes *Discoveries*, a twice-yearly journal for history teachers.

Enquiries about the project, INSET and *Discoveries* should be addressed to the Schools History Project, Trinity and All Saints' College, Brownberrie Lane, Horsforth, Leeds LS18 5HD.

Enquiries about the *Discovering the Past* series should be addressed to the publishers, John Murray.

Series consultants
Terry Fiehn
Tim Lomas
Martin and Jenny Tucker

Pupils' Book ISBN 0–7195–7052–2
Teachers' Evaluation Pack ISBN 0–7195–7053–0

© Colin Shephard, Tim Lomas 1995

First published in 1992 as part of *Societies in Change*
by John Murray (Publishers) Ltd
50 Albemarle Street, London W1X 4BD

This edition first published 1995

Reprinted 1996

Typeset by Wearset, Boldon, Tyne and Wear
Printed in Great Britain by Butler & Tanner Ltd, Frome and London

A CIP record for this book is available from the British Library

S·H·P
THE SCHOOLS HISTORY PROJECT

DISCOVERING THE PAST

DISCOVERING THE
MAKING OF THE UK

CROWN, PARLIAMENTS AND PEOPLES
1500–1750

Colin Shephard (Director, SHP)
Tim Lomas

JOHN MURRAY

cknowledgements

Illustrations by David Anstey, Art Construction, Peter Bull Art Studio.

Illustration on **pp.82–83** reproduced from *The Times London Atlas* by kind permission of Times Books.

Photographs reproduced by kind permission of:
cover: *left* Ashmolean Museum, Oxford. **p.1** Ashmolean Museum, Oxford. **p.3** Kunsthistorisches Museum, Vienna/Bridgeman Art Library. **p.4** *top left* Ms311 Virgil, courtesy of Earl of Leicester, Holkham Hall: Coke Estates; *top right* National Portrait Gallery, London; *centre right* Hulton Picture Company; *bottom left and bottom right* Mansell Collection. **p.5** *top left, top right, bottom left* Mansell Collection; *centre left* by courtesy of the Trustees of the Victoria and Albert Museum/ Bridgeman Art Library; *centre right* Hulton Picture Company. **p.6** *top left and top right* Mansell Collection. **p.7** *centre right and bottom* Mansell Collection. **p.10** Museo e Gallerie Nazionali di Capodimonte, Naples/Bridgeman Art Library, London. **p.11** reproduced by courtesy of the Trustees of the British Museum. **p.12** *top* National Trust Photographic Library/Graham Challifour; *centre right and bottom* Hereford City Council; *centre left* AA Picture Library. **p.13** *top left* A.F.Kersting; *top right* National Trust Photographic Library/Mike Williams; *centre left and bottom left* Museum of London Picture Library; *centre* E.T.Archive; *centre right* by courtesy of the Board of Trustees of the Victoria and Albert Museum; *bottom centre* Cheltenham Art Gallery and Museums, Glos./Bridgeman Art Library, London; *bottom right* Woodmansterne/Reproduced courtesy of the Museum of London. **p.15** *top* A.F.Kersting; *bottom left and right* Plymouth County Council. **p.17** *left* Rijksmuseum, Amsterdam; *right* Alan Jacobs Gallery, London/Bridgeman Art Library, London. **p.18** Mary Evans Picture Library. **p.19** Mary Evans Picture Library. **p.20** *top* Royal London Hospital Trust Archive; *bottom* Bodleian Library, Oxford. **p.21** *top left* Yale Center for British Art, Paul Mellon Collection; *top right* The Tate Gallery, London; *bottom* reproduced by permission of the Marquess of Bath, Longleat House, Warminster, Wiltshire. **p.22** *top* Hulton Picture Company. **p.23** *top* Fitzwilliam Museum, Cambridge; *bottom* Mansell Collection. **p.24** Fotomas Index. **p.26** *top* Sonia Halliday Photographs. **p.28** *top* Mansell Collection; *bottom* Fotomas Index. **p.29** Burghley House, Stamford, Lincolnshire/Bridgeman Art Library, London. **p.31** *top* A.F.Kersting. **p.32** Mansell Collection. **p.34** Michael Holford. **pp.36–37** *top* Mansell Collection. **p.37** *bottom right* Mansell Collection. **p.38** Mansell Collection. **p.40** *left* Peter Newark's Historical Pictures; *centre* Royal Collection, St James's Palace © H.M. the Queen; *right* National Portrait Gallery, London. **p.41** *top left* Wayland Picture Library; *top right* by courtesy of the Board of Trustees

of the Victoria and Albert Museum; *centre right* National Portrait Gallery, London; *centre left* Bodleian Library, Oxford; *bottom* Private Collection/Bridgeman Art Library, London. **p.44** Fotomas Index. **p.45** *top* Hulton Picture Company; *bottom* Fotomas Index. **p.46** Fotomas Index. **p.47** *left* Historical Portraits Ltd, London/Bridgeman Art Library, London; *right* Fotomas Index. **p.48** House of Lords, Westminster, London/Bridgeman Art Library, London. **p.51** *top* Mansell Collection; *bottom* C.M.Dixon. **p.52** The Board of Trustees of the National Museums on Merseyside (Walker Art Gallery). **p.54** *top left* The Board of Trustees of the Royal Armouries; *centre and bottom* Mary Evans Picture Library. **p.55** *top* Mansell Collection; *bottom* Hulton Picture Company. **p.57** Fotomas Index. **pp.58–59** *both* Mansell Collection. **p.61** *top* Ashmolean Museum, Oxford; *centre* by courtesy of the Earl of Rosebery/Scottish National Portrait Gallery; *bottom* Mansell Collection. **p.62** Mansell Collection. **p.63** *left* Royal Collection, St James's Palace © Her Majesty the Queen; *right* Mary Evans Picture Library. **p.64** Fotomas Index. **p.65** Mansell Collection. **p.66** Mansell Collection. **p.67** Private Collection/Bridgeman Art Library, London. **p.68** Bodleian Library, Oxford. **p.69** Fotomas Index. **p.70** National Portrait Gallery, London. **p.71** Fotomas Index. **p.75** Mansell Collection. **p.77** Scottish National Portrait Gallery. **p.78** Tate Gallery, London/Bridgeman Art Library, London. **p.79** *top left and right* Mansell Collection; *bottom* Ann Ronan Picture Library. **p.80** *top left* Mansell Collection; *top right* Ancient Art and Architecture Collection; *bottom* Wellcome Institute Library, London. **p.81** Mansell Collection. **p.83** *bottom* Museum of London Picture Library. **p.84** Mansell Collection. **p.85** E.T.Archive. **p.86** Reproduced by courtesy of the Trustees of the British Museum. **p.87** E.T.Archive. **p.88** *top* British Library, London; *bottom* Agnew and Sons London/Bridgeman Art Library, London. **p.89** *top* Bodleian Library, Oxford; *centre* Hampshire Museum Service; *bottom* Royal Institution of Cornwall, Truro. **p.90** *top* Cheltenham Art Gallery and Museums, Glos./Bridgeman Art Library, London; *centre* City of Bristol Museum and Art Gallery/Bridgeman Art Library, London; *bottom* Paul Harrison/Dyfed County Council Record Office. **p.91** *top left* Honourable Michael Willoughby; *top right* Leeds City Libraries; *bottom* Bodleian Library, Oxford. **p.92** *top and centre* Scottish Ethnological Archive, National Museums of Scotland; *bottom* Leeds City Libraries. **p.93** *bottom* Ulster Folk and Transport Museum; *rest* Mary Evans Picture Library.

Note: The wording and sentence structure of some written sources have been adapted and simplified to make them accessible to all pupils while faithfully preserving the sense of the original.

Contents

N.B. Words in SMALL CAPITALS are defined in the glossary on page 95.

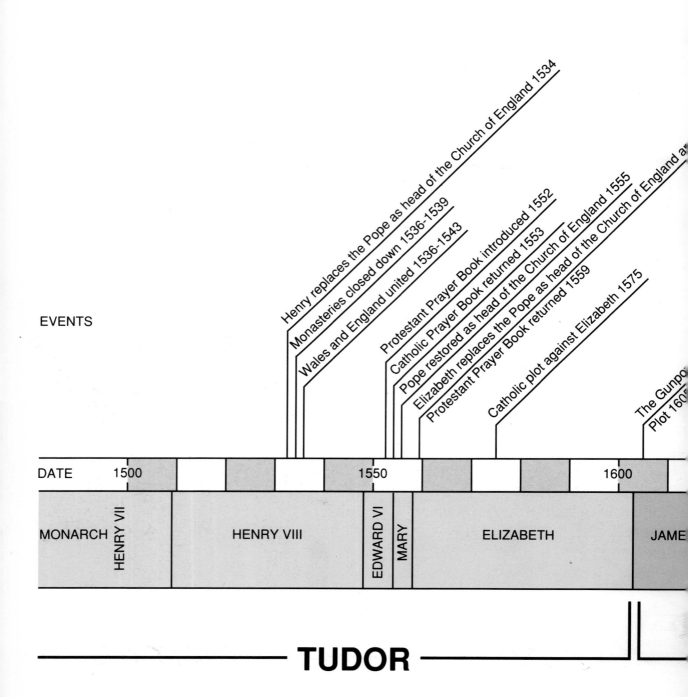

EVENTS

Henry replaces the Pope as head of the Church of England 1534

Monasteries closed down 1536-1539

Wales and England united 1536-1543

Protestant Prayer Book introduced 1552

Catholic Prayer Book returned 1553

Pope restored as head of the Church of England 1555

Elizabeth replaces the Pope as head of the Church of England 1559

Protestant Prayer Book returned 1559

Catholic plot against Elizabeth 1575

The Gunpo
Plot 160

DATE   1500   1550   1600

MONARCH | HENRY VII | HENRY VIII | EDWARD VI | MARY | ELIZABETH | JAME

TUDOR

THE MAKING OF THE UK

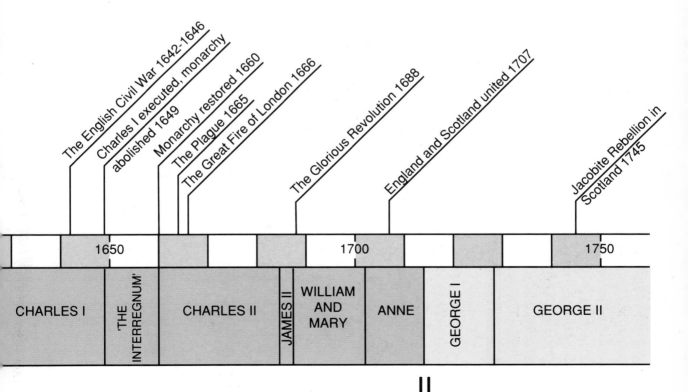

The English Civil War 1642-1646

Charles I executed, monarchy abolished 1649

Monarchy restored 1660

The Plague 1665

The Great Fire of London 1666

The Glorious Revolution 1688

England and Scotland united 1707

Jacobite Rebellion in Scotland 1745

| 1650 | | 1700 | | 1750 |

| CHARLES I | 'THE INTERREGNUM' | CHARLES II | JAMES II | WILLIAM AND MARY | ANNE | GEORGE I | GEORGE II |

STUART — HANOVER

England in the 1500s

IF YOU travelled through England in the 1500s what would you have seen? And how different was it from England today?

In 1500, most of the land had not been altered by humans. There were still huge areas of forest where wild pigs, wild cats and even wolves still lived. Much of the rest of the land was wasteland, covered in scrub and thickets.

Only a small part of the land was farmed. And an even smaller part of this was used for growing crops. Most of the farm land was used for grazing sheep. There were about eight million sheep and only about 2.7 million people! The sheep were kept to supply wool for the cloth industry.

Nine out of ten people still lived in the countryside and worked on the land. Most villagers lived on what they could grow. If they grew more than they needed they sold the surplus in the local market town. For most ordinary villagers it was often a struggle just to keep their family fed. To make a little extra money they did some spinning and weaving.

Cloth making was England's most important industry. Nearly every town had a group of spinners, weavers, fullers and tuckers (who pounded the cloth to make it thicker), and dyers.

Most towns were little more than overgrown villages. The townspeople kept cattle on common land in the town and every week the streets were filled with the noise of cattle coming to market.

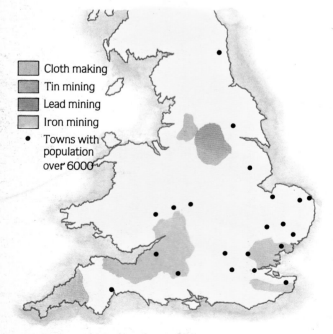

Cloth making
Tin mining
Lead mining
Iron mining
• Towns with population over 6000

SOURCE 1 England in 1500

SOURCE 2 Written in 1577 by William Harrison, who lived in Essex

66 *There are old men living in my village who have noticed three things to be greatly changed.*
One is the many chimneys recently erected.
The second is [the beds]. Their fathers used to sleep on straw on rough mats covered only with a sheet and a good round log under their heads. Pillows were only for women in childbed.
The third is the change from wooden plates and spoons to silver or tin.

SOURCE 3 Richard Carew's description of farmers' houses in Cornwall in the 1580s

66 *Walls of earth, low thatched roofs, few partitions, no glass windows, and scarcely any chimneys other than a hole in the wall to let out the smoke; their bed, straw and a blanket.*

SOURCE 4 A sixteenth-century dinner

66 *The first course:*
- *a collar of brawn*
- *a roasted tongue and udder*
- *a leg of pork, boiled*
- *a piece of roast beef*
- *a venison pasty*
- *a marrow pudding*
- *a goose*
- *a salad*
The second course:
- *two joints of lamb, roasted*
- *a couple of rabbits*
- *a dish of larks*
- *sliced venison, cold*
- *a dish of tarts and custard*
Then serve your cheese and fruit.

---

1. From the information and the sources on this page make a list of differences between England in the 1500s and England today. Use the following headings for your list:
   - population
   - size of towns
   - houses and furniture
   - meals
   - industries
   - jobs
   - the countryside.

Social groups

ne sixteenth-century writer said: 'We in England
ivide our people into four groups: gentlemen,
tizens, yeomen and labourers.' What life was like
epended a great deal on which of these groups you
elonged to.

Gentlemen

Some gentlemen were enormously rich and
owerful. They were dukes and earls. They owned
nd all over England and helped the king run the
ountry.

Other gentlemen were known as 'country
entlemen', or GENTRY. They owned just one estate.
hey had tenant farmers working on their estate.
hey lived comfortably with a large house and
ervants. They also helped in the running of the
ountry. Many were appointed by the king as
JSTICES OF THE PEACE to help run the villages.

Citizens

hese were rich people who lived in the towns. They
rere merchants and master craftsmen. They lived in
ne town houses with servants.

Yeomen

These were farmers who owned land or rented it
from gentlemen. They lived a reasonably
comfortable life.

Labourers

These were people who had no land. If they lived in
the country they worked as farm labourers. If they
lived in the town they might be shopkeepers or
craftsmen such as shoemakers or bricklayers.

---

1. Sources 5–15 below and over the page come
   from the sixteenth century. Study the pictures
   carefully. Write down what you think is
   happening in each picture.
2. For each one say whether you think it shows
   life in a town or in the country.
3. For each one say whether the activity would
   involve gentlemen, citizens, yeomen and/or
   labourers.

SOURCE 5

SOURCE 6

SOURCE 7

SOURCE 8

SOURCE 9

▶ **SOURCE 10**

SOURCE 11

SOURCE 14

SOURCE 15

SOURCE 12

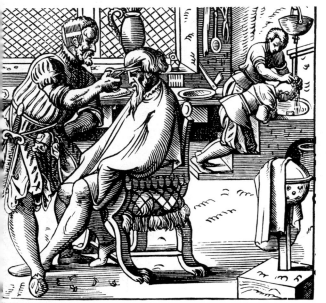

SOURCE 13

Activity

From the following statements choose the one that you most agree with. Explain your choice by referring to Sources 2–15.

- 'Life in this period was unpleasant and hard.'
- 'Life in this period was comfortable and pleasant.'
- 'It is difficult to generalise about what life was like in this period. It depended on who you were and where you were living.'

Were the poor really poor?

IN THE sixteenth and seventeenth centuries one of the most serious worries for the government was the problem of poor people. The towns and roads throughout the country were full of vagrants. These vagrants had no homes or jobs. They wandered around the country begging to keep themselves alive.

A little better off than the vagrants were people who were poor but did at least have somewhere to live and a few belongings. Most of these people worked in the countryside, farming the land. When the harvests were good they just managed to feed their children and look after the old and sick people in their families. But when harvests were bad people had to beg or else starve to death. In Sheffield, for example, in 1616, a third of the population were begging to keep themselves alive.

However, many people in the sixteenth century, and historians since then, claimed that a lot of these vagrants and beggars were not really so helpless. They said the poor could have worked if they had wanted to, but they were deliberately avoiding work and preferred to make their living by begging, robbing and stealing instead.

SOURCE 1 Different types of beggars

A _A Rogue_ will crawl along the streets (supporting his body by a staff) as if there were not strength in his legs: his clothes are all tattered.
Rogues are not driven to this poverty. If they had better clothes they would rather sell them, to move people to pity.

B The **Upright Man** is the king of vagrants. He carries a staff. He doesn't beg, but demands that people give him money. He helps himself to other vagrants' possessions and even to their women.

C The **Counterfeit Crank** pretended to be lame or ill. For example, he would suck soap to make himself foam at the mouth and then he would pretend to have an epileptic fit.

D The **Doxy** carries on her back a great pack in which she has all the things she has stolen. As she walks she knits, and wears a needle in her hat. If any chickens are near she feeds them with bread, and has a thread tied to a hook baited. The chicken swallows this, is choked and is then hidden under her cloak.

E **Clapper dudgeons** lay crowfoot and salt upon the place of the body they wish to make sore. They then put on it a linen cloth till it stick fast. When plucked off it leaves raw flesh. They cast over that a bloody and filthy cloth. With their women they travel from market to market. They are able by begging to get five shillings in a week. They often have six or seven pounds on them.

1. Look at Source 1. Which of beggars 1–8 are described in boxes A–G? Make sure you give your reasons.
2. Which of the drawings in Source 1 were made in the sixteenth century, and which are modern reconstructions?

Activity

Picture 2 in Source 1 shows Nicholas Jennings, a famous vagrant. Your teacher will give you more information about him.

Design a 'Wanted' poster for him. Show what he looked like and why he was dangerous.

The Abraham Man walks with a sheet around his body. He is often bare-armed and bare-legged. He pretends to be mad by whooping and bellowing and staring with a wild look.

F

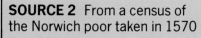

7

8

Bawdy Baskets are women and go with baskets on their arms. In these baskets they have laces, pins and silk of all colours. They will steal linen clothes off hedges. They get from maidservants, when their mistress is out of the way, some good piece of beef, bacon or cheese, that shall be worth 12d, for 2d of their toys.

G

SOURCE 2 From a census of the Norwich poor taken in 1570

"*Anne Buckle, 46 years old. Widow. Two children, one 9 years old, the other 5 years old, that work lace. Have always lived here. Very poor.*

John Burr, 54 years old. Glazier. Very sick and cannot work. Alice his wife that spins. Seven children, the eldest 20 years of age, the youngest 2 years. They can spin wool. Have always lived here. Very poor."

3. What evidence can you find that not everyone in Source 1 was poor and helpless?
4. Why do you think so many people pretended to be poor and helpless?
5. Can you find anyone in Sources 1 and 2 who you think was really poor and helpless? Give your reasons.

The houses of the poor

SOURCE 3 The inside of a farm worker's cottage

When someone died an inventory was made of their possessions. Where these inventories have survived they are useful for helping us work out how rich someone was.

SOURCE 4 The inventory of Thomas Herries, who died in 1599

"*1 boarded bedstead, 1 mattress, 1 bolster, 1 pillow, 1 pair of sheets, 1 bed blanket.*

2 salt boxes, 1 frying pan, 1 pair of tongs and a roasting iron, 1 kettle, 1 saw, 3 spoons, 2 wooden plates, 5 dishes and 2 earthen pots, 1 stone pot.

A little table, 2 stools, 3 chisels and 2 hammers, 2 pairs of hand cuffs and 1 dozen handkerchiefs, 2 old shirts."

1. Compare Sources 3 and 4. Who do you think was poorer: Thomas Herries or the people in Source 3?

WERE THE POOR REALLY POOR?

Why were people poor?

In the sixteenth century the ruling classes were certain they knew why there were so many poor people.

> **SOURCE 5** Some of the ruling class's views
>
> ❝■ In 1594 William Lambarde, who worked for the government, said that the number of people in England was growing because people of all classes freely married and had children. This made food scarce and put prices up.
>
> ■ In 1596 Edward Hext, a Justice of the Peace, said that the poor were lazy. They would do anything to avoid work. They would risk being hanged rather than work. ❞

> **SOURCE 7** A modern historian summarising the position of the poor in the sixteenth century
>
> ❝The situation grew worse during the sixteenth century. Henry VIII had closed the monasteries, which had helped to look after the poor.
>
> Many landowners had enclosed [fenced off] common land on their manor and used it themselves. So poor villagers now had nowhere to graze their animals.
>
> Some landowners stopped growing crops altogether. There was a big demand for wool, so they took up sheep farming instead. This meant fewer jobs.
>
> Prices were going up faster than wages and people's pay didn't buy as much as it used to. The poor were getting poorer.❞

1. Look at Source 5. Who do Lambarde and Hext blame for the large numbers of poor and unemployed?
2. Does the modern historian in Source 7 agree with them?
3. Can you think of reasons why Sources 5 and 7 disagree?
4. Look at Source 6 . Which decade would have been the worst to live in?
5. How does Source 6 help you to understand why there were so many poor people?

Activity

You are Edward Hext, a JUSTICE OF THE PEACE in Somerset in 1596. You have been appointed as a JP by the queen. You are the most important local official in your village. It is your job to keep law and order, to punish vagrants and to look after the helpless poor.

Use Sources 1–7 to write a report to the government. Explain why there are so many poor people, the problems they are causing and what you think should be done about it.

Your teacher will give you a copy of a real report by Hext. Don't copy it, just use it for some ideas.

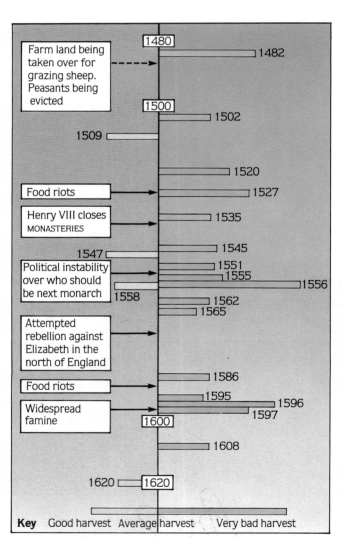

SOURCE 6 Events and developments that affected the poor, 1480–1620

Key Good harvest Average harvest Very bad harvest

What did the government do about the poor?

As you'll have seen from the previous activity, in the sixteenth century there were:
- people who were too sick, too old or too crippled to work
- people who were fit and willing to work but could not find any work
- people who were fit but were deliberately avoiding work.

1. Do you think all these people should be treated in the same way?
2. Look at Source 8. It shows what the king's government did about the poor. Did the government treat all three groups in the same way in 1547?
3. Did they treat all three groups in the same way in 1601?
4. According to Source 8, did the government's treatment of the poor get gradually better between 1531 and 1601? Explain your answer.
5. Source 9 shows a scene in the mid-sixteenth century. Use Source 8 to work out what offence the men at A and B may have committed.
6. ■ 'The government was cruel and nasty to punish people like this.' Do you agree?

SOURCE 8 Between 1531 and 1601 the government passed many laws relating to the poor throughout the country. These are the most important

❝ *1531 If any man or woman being whole in body be vagrant and can give no explanation how he lawfully gets his living, he shall be tied to the end of a cart, naked, and be beaten with whips throughout the town till his body be bloody. He shall then return to the place where he was born.*

1547 Anyone unemployed for three days was termed a vagrant, and could be branded with a 'V' and given as a slave for two years to the person who reported him to be vagrant.

In return for bread and water he had to do everything his master told him. If he refused he could be whipped and even imprisoned with iron rings around his neck and legs. If a slave ran away twice he could be executed.

1572 Vagrants should be whipped and bored through the ear for a first offence; executed for a third offence.

Everyone in a parish shall make compulsory weekly payments to help the poor and sick.

1576 Parishes should provide raw materials for the unemployed to work with.

1601 Vagrants were to be whipped until they were bloody, then sent to the parish where they were born. There they were placed in work if able-bodied, or in almshouses if not. Persistent vagrants were to be put in a house of correction.

Each parish had to appoint overseers of the poor and had to tax people in the parish to provide materials to set the poor to work. People who failed to pay this tax could go to prison. ❞

SOURCE 9

WERE THE POOR REALLY POOR?

What did the towns do about the poor?

Although the government made laws for all of England, it was the JPs and officials in the towns who actually had to deal with the problem of poverty. Sources 10–14 show some of the actions taken in three large towns in the sixteenth century.

> **SOURCE 10** Four great 'hospitals' for the poor were set up in London in the sixteenth century. John Stow describes two of them
>
> 66*Christ's Hospital in Newgate market [founded in about 1540]: poor fatherless children are there brought up and fed at the expense of the citizens.*
>
> *Bridewell [founded in about 1550] is a workhouse for the poor and idle persons of the city, where a great number of vagrant persons are now set to work and fed at the expense of the citizens.*99

> **SOURCE 11** From the records of Ipswich in 1557
>
> 66*No children shall be permitted to beg. Those adults who are allowed to beg shall have badges.*99

> **SOURCE 12** From the records of Norwich in 1571
>
> 66*There shall be a work place for the men to grind malt and the women to spin. These persons shall work for their meat and drink. Those that refuse to work are to be punished by the whip.*99

> **SOURCE 13** From the records of Ipswich, 1591
>
> 66*The town's clothiers shall set the poor to work.*

> **SOURCE 14** From Norwich parish records from 1598–9: payments relating to the poor
>
> 66*Paid to those who are very sick* £2 7s 3d
> *Paid for the keeping of two of Bradley's children* £3
> *Paid for nursing a young infant left in the parish one week* 1s 8d
> *Paid for putting Thomas Clarke out as an apprentice* 9s 1d
> *Paid to the constables for sending away vagrants* 4s 8d

1. What did Norwich, Ipswich and London do about:
   - people who were unable to work, such as the sick and the young
   - people who were fit and wanted to work
   - people who were deliberately avoiding work?
2. Did the towns look after the poor better than the government did?

SOURCE 15 Blind people, painted in the sixteenth century

3. Look at Source 15. Do you think the artist wants you to feel sympathy for these people?
4. Does the artist show these people to be really helpless or just pretending to be helpless?

Did things improve in the seventeenth and eighteenth centuries?

The Poor Laws that were in place by 1601 were the basis for the government's policy for the next 200 years. But how about the towns? Did things get better or worse for the poor?

SOURCE 16 A general description by a modern historian

In the seventeenth century harvests failed, on average, every four years. Faced with hunger many of the poor left their homes and travelled to towns, especially London — which grew to be the biggest city in Europe by 1700. Others went to the forests where they set up simple homes, stole fuel and carved out fields. But soon even these areas became cramped and a new trend appeared, as many people emigrated: 200,000 went to America in the seventeenth century.

SOURCE 17 From the Surrey Quarter Sessions Book of 1667

Robert Wheeler is destitute, his house being lately blown down. It is ordered that the Overseers of the parish may erect a cottage on the wast [wasteland] for the said Wheeler, the cottage to be kept for the use of the poor of the parish.

SOURCE 18 From parish records of Chalfont St Peter, Buckinghamshire, recording the help given to George Monk between 1748 and 1759

1748	Paid for 2 shirts for G. Monk	5s 6d
1750	Paid to Jane Garman for looking after Monk in the cage	2s
1752	Paid for a waistcoat and shirt and breeches for GM	7s 6d
	Bought him a new kettle	1s 6d
1754	Bought him a tin pot and 2 knives	8d
	Paid for a lock and chain for G. Monk	5s 6d
1759	Paid for 2 handkerchiefs	7d

▶ **SOURCE 19** Guy's Hospital in London. It was founded in 1720 for the care of poor people who were ill by a rich London bookseller, Thomas Guy. It was called one of the greatest hospitals ever founded by a member of the public

SOURCE 20 From the Cornwall Quarter Sessions in 1741

Thomas Davy, a vagrant, has been judged an incorrigible rogue. He is remanded to the prison to serve with hard labour for three months and also on Saturday next he is to be stripped naked from his middle upwards and be publicly whipped at Truro till his body be bloody.

1. Look at Source 19. How have the designers of the hospital tried to look after the needs of poor patients?
2. Do Sources 16–20 suggest the poor were treated more or less kindly in the seventeenth century than they were in the sixteenth century? Give reasons for your answer.
3. Draw a timeline from 1500 to 1750. Mark in changes to the treatment of the poor mentioned on pages 8–11. Did things always get better? Choose two examples to support your answer.
4. Which was the single most important change introduced in the treatment of the poor?

One of the Rooms for Necessarys below Stairs.

The Grand Stair Case

A Prospect of one of the Wards.

Were the rich really rich?

YOU probably do not consider yourself to be rich. But do most people today have a better standard of living than rich people in the sixteenth and seventeenth centuries?

1. Make a list of all the rooms in your house or flat.
2. Make a list of the main items of furniture and equipment in your house or flat.
3. What do you think are the five most useful items on your list — ones your family could not easily manage without? Compare your list with lists made by other people in the class.

The houses of the rich

1. Sources 1—4 show pictures of rooms as they might have looked during the sixteenth and seventeenth centuries. See if you can match up the following captions with the correct rooms:
   - Bedroom
   - Kitchen
   - Long Gallery
   - Dining room.
2. Which of these rooms do you have in your house or flat?
3. Choose one of these rooms. Compare it with a room in your home. What are the similarities? What are the differences? Which one would you rather live in, and why?
4. All the rooms in Sources 1—4 are found in the houses shown in Sources 5 and 6. See if you can match them up. Explain your choice.

SOURCE 1

SOURCE 2

SOURCE 3

SOURCE 4

SOURCE 5 The Old House, Hereford

SOURCE 6 Hardwick Hall, Derbyshire

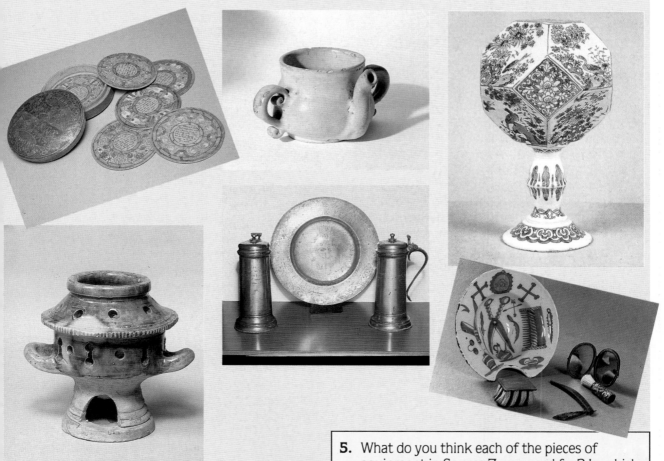

SOURCE 7 Some household objects from the period 1500–1750

5. What do you think each of the pieces of equipment in Source 7 was used for? In which rooms would they be used?
6. Would any of the items in Source 7 be useful today?

WERE THE RICH REALLY RICH?

Changes

For many rich people the sixteenth century was a time of peace and prosperity. Many new houses were built. Some of these new houses were now built of brick, instead of wood.

Inside, many of the rooms had wooden panels on the walls instead of the tapestries which had been used in medieval times.

Fireplaces became more usual, even in smaller rooms. Kitchens often had a large fireplace. Dogs were sometimes bred to run inside a wheel that turned a spit in front of the fire. Hot ashes were put in the dog's wheel to make it run faster.

People's living habits were changing. They wanted more privacy, so they no longer all lived together in a large hall. There were separate rooms for resting, sleeping and eating.

In the seventeenth century these changes continued. Floors were usually made of wood, though cobbles or stones were still used in the servants' areas. Ceilings in the main living rooms were plastered, often with delicate patterns. The rich slept in four-poster beds, although generally people had a lot less furniture than we do today.

There were few bathrooms. Baths were often taken in the bedroom. Most people used a toilet that was nothing more than a wooden seat over a bucket. The contents were thrown onto the land around the house or into nearby streams.

People's habits were different to ours. Spitting was common. Nobody was allowed to leave the table while a meal was still in progress. Some people would urinate in their boots because they could not leave the table! The main meal in the sixteenth century was usually about midday, but by the seventeenth century breakfast at around 9.00 a.m. and supper at 10.00 p.m. were more popular.

---

1. Write down five ways in which houses and life inside them had changed for rich people since the Middle Ages.

Activity

Design an advertisement for the wheel-turned spit mentioned above. Show what you think it looked like and how it worked, and explain its advantages.

A tradeswoman's house

Throughout the sixteenth and seventeenth centuries towns were growing. The number of middle-class people such as traders, craftsmen, doctors and lawyers was also increasing. They had done well in business and had more money than they needed for the basic necessities of life.

Source 8 is the inventory of the house of Mary Meighan of Shrewsbury. She died in 1660.

SOURCE 8 From the inventory of Mary Meighan

In the kitchen: 2 small tables. 1 cupboard. 1 bench. 2 chairs. 4 small stools and all the panelling. 1 large screen on glass. 3 shelves to hold books.

In the parlour: 2 tables. 1 cupboard. 2 benches. 3 joint stools. 2 small carpets. 1 cupboard cloth. 8 cushions and all the panelling. 1 chair. Pewter. Iron ware.

In the chamber over the parlour: 1 small table. 1 bench. 1 chest. 1 standing bedstead. 1 truckle bed [a small bed on wheels]. 1 twin chair. 1 feather bed. 1 flock bed. 2 bolsters. 2 blankets. 2 pillows. 1 covering, curtains and valance for 1 bed. 1 panelled door.

In the chamber over the kitchen: 2 standing beds. 1 wardrobe. 2 chests. 3 coffers. Panelling. Bedding, curtains, valance, linen ware.

In the room on the stair head: 1 little cupboard and 1 truckle bed. 1 basin. 1 door with panelling. Bedding. Clothing.

In the tanhouse: 82 tanned hides. 6 horse hides. Dozen calf skins. 4 loads of bark. 1 lead pump. 1 bark mill. 3 gutters. 2 tubs. All other tanning implements. 1 cow and 1 hog. Charcoal.

In the servants' chamber: 1 flock bed and clothes. 4 silver spoons. Hemp and flax.

---

1. Can you work out how many rooms there were in Mary Meighan's house?
2. What was each room used for?
3. Draw a plan of the house showing the rooms and the furniture. We do not know what this house actually looked like, so it is not possible for your plan to be 'right'. Compare your plan with others in the class.
4. What trade did Mary Meighan carry out? Give three reasons for your answer.

A merchant's house

Sources 9–11 are pictures of a house built at the end of the sixteenth century by a Plymouth merchant. Plymouth was a busy port and one of the most important towns in England at this time.

1. Look at the three pictures, Sources 9–11. What are the main differences between living in this house and in your house today? Which do you prefer?
2. Do you think the merchant living in this house was as rich as the people living in the houses in Sources 5 and 6 on page 13? Explain your answer.

(houses in Sources 5 and 6 on page 13)

Activity

You are an 'estate agent' in the sixteenth century. It is your job to advertise this house for sale. Design a leaflet. (It might help you to look at estate agents' adverts from your local newspaper. But remember, people in the sixteenth century would expect a different kind of house to people today.)

SOURCE 9

▲ **SOURCE 10**

SOURCE 11

Activity

If people from the sixteenth century had to leave five things in a time capsule to show people hundreds of years later what their lives were like, what would be the best five things for a) a rich person, and b) a poor person? Explain your choice.

Private lives

MUCH of this book is about the actions of governments and kings and queens, but just as important are the private lives of people and their families.

However, it is very difficult to find evidence about people's private lives in the past – about the relationships between husband and wife, and between parents and children, for example.

1. In 100 years' time historians will want to study us and what our lives are like in the 1990s. Make a list of ten different types of source (e.g. diaries or furniture) they would find useful for working out what you eat, what you do in your spare time, what you wear and what your home is like.
2. You may have included TV advertisements in your list. How reliable would these be in telling a future historian about what we eat and wear?
3. Do you think people from the sixteenth and seventeenth centuries have left sources, similar to the ones in your list, which we can study? Give reasons for your answer.
4. Much of the evidence on the next six pages comes from diaries and autobiographies. Why should we be careful about believing everything someone says in a diary or an autobiography?

Getting married

One historian, Lawrence Stone, has argued that between 1500 and 1750 important changes took place in people's private lives. Read pages 16–19 and see if you think the evidence supports his views.

At the beginning of the sixteenth century parents arranged the marriages of their children, who had no say in who they were going to marry.
By the end of the period young people getting married did have a say in who they would marry and sometimes even married for love.

SOURCE 1 How Elizabeth Paston was treated by her mother, when her family disagreed about who she should be married to (from family letters in the mid-fifteenth century). The Pastons were a middle-class family

> She has since Easter usually been beaten once or twice in the week, and sometimes twice in a day, and had her head broken in two or three places.

SOURCE 2 An extract from William Shaftoe's will, 1599. He was a rich farmer

> To my daughter, Margerie, 50 sheep, and I bestow her in marriage upon Edward son of Reynold Shaftoe.

SOURCE 3 From the diary of Ralph Josselin, a seventeenth-century clergyman. The first extract describes the occasion when he first saw the woman whom he later married. The incident took place in church

> **1639** My eye was fixed with love upon a maid and hers upon me, who afterwards became my wife.
> **1681** Mary [Josselin's daughter] rejected Mr Rhea. Her reasons were many. His age: being fourteen years older, she might be left a widow with children. His estate: which is not more than £350 a year, plus his salary as rector of £100. He seemed to her not loving. It was no small grief to me, but I could not desire it, when she said it would make both their lives miserable.

SOURCE 4 In 1719 the aristocratic Duke of Richmond arranged a marriage for his son

> The marriage was made to cancel a gambling debt; the young people's consent having been the last thing thought of. The boy was sent for from school and the young lady from the nursery; a clergyman was in attendance and they were told they were immediately to become man and wife. The young lady did not utter a word, the young boy exclaimed, 'They are surely not going to marry me to that dowdy!'

SOURCE 5 In 1641 Charles I's daughter Mary, aged nine, was married to Prince William of Orange, aged fifteen. The marriage was arranged by her father

SOURCE 7 A wedding feast, painted in 1568

SOURCE 6 'Wife sales' were common amongst the ordinary people. It was a kind of divorce. Both husband and wife agreed to it and the wife would agree to the new husband. This is a description written in the 1740s

The husband puts a halter about her neck and leads her to the next market place, and there puts her up to auction to be sold to the best bidder, as if she were a brood mare. A purchaser is usually arranged beforehand.

SOURCE 8 Written by Lawrence Stone

Among the poorer people children were much freer to choose their husbands and wives. Some children left home as young as ten years old. Most left home by the time they were seventeen to become apprentices, domestic servants or live-in labourers in other people's houses. They were free of parental control. The only thing that held them back was the need for enough money to set up house. This was the main reason why they did not marry until their middle twenties.

1. Draw a timeline to cover the years 1450–1750. Mark on it the following names and dates: Elizabeth Paston, 1450; Margerie Shaftoe, 1599; Ralph Josselin, 1639; Princess Mary, 1641; Mary Josselin, 1681; the Duke of Richmond's son, 1719; the wife sale, 1740.
2. Beside each entry on your timeline, mark whether that person chose who they should marry, or had the person chosen for her/him. You will find the evidence in Sources 1–6.
3. Does this timeline show Stone to be right?
4. Suppose you wanted to choose sources which showed Stone to be right. Which ones would you choose? Explain your choice.

SOURCE 9 Average age when married in the sixteenth century

Upper-class daughters	*20*
Upper-class sons	*21*
Lower-class daughters	*25 to 27*
Lower-class sons	*27 to 28*

5. Describe what is happening in Source 7 in as much detail as you can.
6. From Sources 1–9 pick two reasons for getting married and two reasons for not getting married. Do you think they are good reasons? Are any of them still used today?

PRIVATE LIVES

Being married

> At the beginning of the sixteenth century husband and wife did not have a loving relationship. They spent little time together. Husbands were masters over their wives and had little affection for them. The main purpose of wives was to produce male heirs.
> By the eighteenth century husbands and wives were more affectionate and loved each other more. They were also more equal and spent more time together.

One problem we have in finding out about marriages in this period is that although just over half the population was female we know little about what women thought and felt. Much of our evidence about what women were like and about relationships between husbands and wives comes from the husbands!

Men believed that they were best at making decisions, at action and business, while women were meant to be maternal, domestic and obedient. Married women had few rights — as soon as they got married everything they owned became their husband's. A husband had the right to beat his wife, as long as the stick was no thicker than a man's thumb.

SOURCE 10 A scold's bridle. This was used as a punishment for nagging wives in the sixteenth century

1. Look at Source 10. How do you think the scold's bridle worked?

SOURCE 11 Men's views of women
a) An extract from a sermon Bishop Aylmer gave to Queen Elizabeth

> Women are of two sorts: some of them are wiser, better learned and more constant than a number of men, but some are foolish, wanton, flibbergibs, tattlers, witless, feeble, proud, dainty, tale-bearers, rumour-raisers and in everyway doltified with the dregs of the devil's dunghill.

b) Extracts from the Homily on Marriage. This had to be read in church every Sunday from 1562

> Woman is the weaker vessel, of a frail heart, inconstant, and with a word soon stirred to anger.

2. What do you think these terms from Source 11 mean: flibbergibs, tattlers?
3. If you were a man in this period how would you use Source 11 to explain why you had the right to be in charge of your wife?

But were marriages really like this, with the wife doing as she was told all the time? Let's look at two marriages from the seventeenth century.

SOURCE 12 Extracts from the diary of Samuel Pepys

> **2 May 1663** I slept till almost 7 o'clock. So up and to my office (having had some angry words with my wife about her neglecting to keep the house clean, I calling her a 'beggar' and she calling me a 'prick-louse'). Returned home to dinner. Very merry and well pleased with my wife.
> **19 December 1664** I was very angry and began to find fault with my wife for not commanding the servants as she ought. She gave me an angry answer. I did strike her over her left eye such a blow, as the poor wretch did cry out. But her spirit was such that she scratched and bit me.
> **12 July 1667** . . . And so home, and there finding my wife in a bad mood for my not dining at home, I did give her a pull by the nose. I decided to go back to the office to avoid further anger. She followed me in a devilish manner, so I got her into the garden out of hearing (to avoid shame) and managed to calm her. Then I walked with her in the garden, and so to supper, pretty good friends, and so to bed.

4. How would you describe the marriage in Source 12: stormy, peaceful, boring, loving?
5. How accurate do you think Pepys' account is? Write Elizabeth Pepys' version.

SOURCE 13 Lucy Hutchinson wrote this to her children, after her husband died. In the style of the time she calls herself 'she'

He managed the reins of government with love and she delighted in his government. He governed by persuasion. So generous was he to her that he would never receive an account of what she had spent. So constant was he in his love that when she ceased to be young and lovely he began to show most fondness. 99

6. Find three differences between the marriages in Sources 12 and 13. Who was more equal with her husband, Lucy Hutchinson or Elizabeth Pepys?
7. Who would you rather have been, Lucy Hutchinson or Elizabeth Pepys?
8. Pepys' diary was written just for himself. Lucy's account was written to tell her children about their father. Which account do you think is the more reliable?

One of the reasons suggested by historians to explain why husbands and wives were not very close was that marriages were so short. Marriage was a very temporary arrangement. The death of one of the partners usually ended it before their children were very old. Most couples had only a year or two together by themselves. By 1750 this situation had changed. Marriages lasted longer.

SOURCE 14 A Frenchman's view of English marriages in 1741

Three marriages out of four are based upon affection. To have a wife who is not agreeable to you must, in England, make life a misery because husband and wife live constantly together. The Englishman makes more effort to get to know his bride before marriage. This is the reason why marriage before the age of 25 is rare. 99

Privacy

Lawrence Stone has supported his argument that marriages became closer by examining changes in the design of houses. At the beginning of the sixteenth century the rich lived in big houses. Husband and wife each had their own separate rooms and their own servants. They spent little time together.

The houses had no corridors. The bedrooms were interlocking. To get from one side of the house to the other you had to go through other people's rooms. Family members had no chance to live privately — servants and guests might come wandering through at any moment.

But by the seventeenth century larger houses were built with corridors. The bedrooms were upstairs with the living rooms downstairs.

Having children

In the sixteenth century about one in five of all babies died before their first birthday. There were many reasons for this: clumsy delivery of the baby at birth, neglect, and the dirt and squalor many babies were brought up in.

SOURCE 15 A sixteenth-century engraving

1. Look at Source 15. The mother has only just given birth to her child. What dangers can you see to the newborn baby?

PRIVATE LIVES

Parents in the sixteenth century tried not to get emotionally involved with their children because they expected them to die. It was common to give a newborn child the same first name as one that had just died. It was seen as a replacement.

Most rich mothers sent their babies to 'wet nurses' until they were about eighteen months old. The death rates for these babies was twice as high as for babies who stayed with their mothers.

Babies were often bound in swaddling clothes for at least the first four months. They could not move their head or limbs. This was supposed to make babies' limbs grow straight, but it also meant the babies did not need constant attention. They could even be left hanging on pegs. Babies could be left for hours to wallow in their own excrement. Many parents would not even let older children crawl about because they thought this was behaving like an animal.

Children as young as three or four were dressed as little adults. Daughters in rich families were encased in corsets reinforced with iron. This was intended to make sure they walked gracefully, but their lungs were sometimes damaged. Parents aimed to turn children into adults as quickly as possible. Beatings were common and many children grew up fearing their parents.

---

1. Make a list of ten bad things about how children were treated in the sixteenth century.

By 1750 the death rate for babies was falling. Fewer babies died during birth. Better designed forceps were used, rather than the hooked instruments used before.

Childcare was generally improving. It became more common for mothers to breast-feed their babies. Wet nursing was criticised. Swaddling was used less as well. Parents wanted to cuddle their children, which you cannot do if they are swaddled. Parents grieved when young babies died. Children were seen as being different from adults.

---

2. Look at Sources 16–25. Do they show improvements in childcare compared with the sixteenth century?

SOURCE 16 Information taken from the autobiography of Sir Simonds D'Ewes about his childhood. D'Ewes came from a rich family

December 1602 – bungled delivery damaged his right eye at birth – could never use it for reading.
5 months old – sent to wet nurse for several months.
1–8 years old – sent to grandfather's house. Grandparents not there so brought up by servants – parents only visited him twice.
8 years old – sent to boarding school.

SOURCE 17 William Blundell, a member of the gentry, reports the birth and immediate death of his sixth daughter (his ninth child) in 1653

My wife has much disappointed my hopes by bringing forth a daughter, which, finding itself not so welcome in this world as a son, hath departed.

SOURCE 18 A set of seventeenth-century instruments used during childbirth

SOURCE 19 A wet nurse, drawn in 1664

SOURCE 20 A family group around 1645. The father is looking at four skulls in the background which represent his dead children

SOURCE 21 Extracts from the account book of the Countess of Sutherland, 1652. They show the things she bought for her young children

1652

For Margaret a rattle	4s
For James a drum	14s
For Meg a doll	13s 4d

SOURCE 22 Lord Cobham and his family, painted in the sixteenth century

SOURCE 23 The Cholmondley sisters and their babies, painted in the seventeenth century

SOURCE 24 From a book on childcare written by Dr Cadogan in 1748. It includes this strong criticism of how wet nurses looked after babies

66 *When [the baby] cries, he is hung from a nail like a bundle of old clothes and while the nurse attends to her business the child remains thus crucified. All who have been found in this situation had a purple face because the blood could not circulate. The baby was believed to be content because he did not have the strength to cry out.* 99

SOURCE 25 Thomas Coram's reasons for setting up the London Foundling Hospital in 1741. In the first four years 15,000 children were brought to the hospital

66 *To prevent the frequent murders of poor miserable children at their birth and to take in children dropped in churchyards or in the streets.* 99

Activity

In groups, design a magazine for parents living in the early eighteenth century. You will need to refer to all the information on pages 16–21. It might also help if you look at similar magazines which are published now for parents.

Think of the features you could include in your magazine, e.g. adverts for new toys, a famous person of the time writing about their own childhood, an investigation into poor children, a discussion between a man and a woman about their roles in marriage, a questionnaire to find out whether people are happy in their marriage, or a feature on how family life has changed since 1500.

Choose and write one feature each.

Could you enjoy yourself in the sixteenth and seventeenth centuries?

NOWADAYS we take it for granted that a big part of our lives is spent on entertainment, sport or games. Was it different in the sixteenth and seventeenth centuries?

Look at Sources 1–7, which describe popular entertainments of the time.

SOURCE 1 Entertainments described by Edwarde Chamberlayne in the seventeenth century

In their variety of sports and recreation no nation doth excel the English.

The nobility and gentry have their parks, warrens, decoys, horse races, hunting, coursing, fishing, hawking, lurchers, cock-fighting, guns for birding, low bells, bat fowling, angling, nets, tennis, bowling, billiards, stage plays, masques, dancing, singing and all sorts of musical instruments . . .

The citizens and peasants have handball, football, skittles, shovel board, stoolball, goffe, trollmadam, cudgels, bear-baiting, bull-baiting, bow and arrow, shuttlecock, bowling, quoits, leaping, wrestling, pitching the bar and ringing the bells.

► **SOURCE 2** A woodcut from 1636 showing the Cotswold 'Olimpick games', started in 1604, then held annually at Whitsuntide except when they were banned by the Puritans

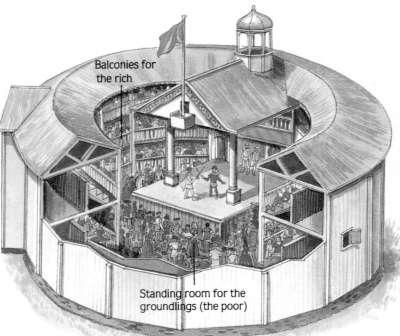

Balconies for the rich

Standing room for the groundlings (the poor)

1. Look at Source 2. Can you find the following: pitching the bar; throwing the sledgehammer; leaping; shin-kicking (with iron-tipped boots); sword-fighting; cudgels; head stands; feasting; fox hunting; hare coursing; dancing to the bagpipes; fireworks (gunfire from a specially built wooden castle)?

◄ **SOURCE 3** The Globe Theatre in London. Going to the theatre became very popular in the sixteenth century with both the rich and the poor

2. Look at Source 1. What do you think the following involved: coursing; trollmadam; stoolball; cudgels? Here are some descriptions to choose from:
   - the aim was to draw blood by a good hefty blow on the scalp
   - dogs chasing a hare around a field
   - a game like cricket, using a stool as a wicket
   - a board game like bagatelle, played by women, where balls were pushed into holes.

3. Which of these statements can be supported by Sources 1, 2 and 3?
   - 'Poor people in the seventeenth century preferred different types of entertainment to rich people.'
   - 'People in the seventeenth century did very little work.'
   - 'Sports and games played in the seventeenth century were different from sports and games today.'

SOURCE 6 Morris dancing in 1600

SOURCE 7 From Misson's *Memoirs and Observations*, written in the late seventeenth century

66 *They tie a rope to the horns of the bull and fasten the other end to an iron ring fixed to a stake. When the sport begins they let loose one of the dogs. The dog runs round the bull, trying to get beneath his belly. Soon the bull beats the ground with his feet.*

The bull's chief aim is not to gore the dog but to slide a horn under the dog's belly and to throw it so high it will break its neck in the fall. This often happens. Sometimes the dog is thrown 30 feet high and this puts him in danger of a damnable squelch when he comes down. 99

SOURCE 4 A public execution in 1641

4. Which of the entertainments in Sources 1–7 are still popular today?
5. Which would not be allowed today?
6. ■ 'People at this time loved violent and dangerous entertainments.'
   Choose three examples from Sources 1–7 to support this statement and three to oppose it.

SOURCE 5 From the diary of Samuel Pepys

21 December 1663 *To Shoe Lane to see a cock-fight at a new pit there. To see the strange variety of people, and all these fellows cursing and betting. It is strange to see how people of this poor rank shall bet £3 or £4 at a time and lose it and yet bet as much at the next battle.* 99

Activity
You are planning the entertainments for your village feast day. Take one or more of the entertainments in Sources 1–7 and make a poster to advertise them. Think about who it would appeal to, and why they might like it.

The Puritans

In the early 1600s a group of hardline Protestants, called PURITANS, tried to stamp out some of the most popular entertainments of the time. Puritans believed in a simple religion and a simple lifestyle — they dressed plainly and believed you had to work hard if you wanted to go to Heaven when you died. They also believed that Sunday was the most important day of the week, and that on Sundays and other holy days people should devote themselves entirely to God. Source 8 was drawn by the Puritans to show what they thought people should and shouldn't do on Sundays.

SOURCE 8 An engraving made by Puritans in 1639

1. Look at Source 8. Describe what is happening in each scene.
2. The Puritans called the pictures on one side 'the works of darkness' and the ones on the other side 'the works of light'. Which do you think is which?

   Local Puritan campaigners managed to ban local festivals, such as the Cotswold Olimpicks (Source 2) or the Whitsuntide Festival at Lyme Regis in Dorset, which dated back to the Middle Ages. But as the Puritans became a powerful force in Parliament a series of acts which affected the whole country was passed:

- to suppress horse racing, cock-fighting, bear-baiting and any unlawful assemblies
- to enforce existing laws against drunkenness and wearing
- to close down theatres, gambling dens and brothels
- to reduce the number of alehouses
- to ban games and sports on Sundays — even going for a walk, except for walking to church.

   What were the Puritans worried about? Sources 9–12 are all written by Puritans in pamphlets or reports about entertainments.

SOURCE 9 Philip Stubbes – a Puritan campaigner – describes a spring festival in 1583

They have twenty or forty pairs of oxen . . . which draw home this maypole (this stinking idol, rather) and they stand it up with handkerchiefs and flags streaming from the top. Then they feast and leap and dance about it as the heathen people did at the dedication of their idols.

SOURCE 10 Philip Stubbes describes a game of football

Sometimes their necks are broken, sometimes their backs, sometimes their legs, sometimes their arms. Sometimes their noses gush out blood. Sometimes their eyes start out. . . . Even the best is wounded, crazed and bruised so that he dieth of it.

SOURCE 11 By George Fox, a Puritan campaigner, in the mid-sixteenth century

Their wakes, feast days, may-games, sports, plays and shows led people away from the fear of God. The days set forth for holy days were usually the times when they most dishonoured God by those things.

SOURCE 12 From a report to the Speaker of the House of Commons from Dorset in 1647

Under the pretence of playing football and cudgel playing and the like there have lately been suspicious meetings and assemblies at several places, made up of disaffected persons, and more such are planned.

3. Are Sources 9–12 reliable in telling us what entertainments were really like in the seventeenth century?
4. What do the writers not like about the entertainments? Try to find at least one different criticism in each source.
5. Would the Puritans' laws affect poor people or rich people more? Refer back to Source 1 if you need to.
6. Which type of source did you find most useful for telling you about Puritan attitudes: the picture (Source 8) or the written sources (Sources 9–12)?

Activity

Divide into groups of five people. You are going to consider whether the period 1500–1750 was a good time to be living in England.

Each person in the group should choose one of the following:
- wives
- rich people
- poor people
- husbands
- children

and draw up at least three statements about the lives of that group which can be supported by evidence on pages 2–25.

Write down all the statements, then add drawings and diagrams to create a wall display on the subject 'Was this a good time to be living in England?'.

Was the Catholic Church still healthy in 1500?

IN 1500 England was a Catholic country. If you were a Christian (and just about everybody was), then you were a Catholic.

You will know how important religion was to people in the Middle Ages. When you were born your parents would have you baptised as soon as possible. This cleaned you of sin. Within a few years you were confirmed and accepted as a member of the Church. If you got married the wedding was carried out by the local priest. And when you were dying the priest gave you the last rites, which released you from your sins.

Even after you died the Church still had a role to play. After death some people were doomed to stay in Hell forever. But even those who were going to Heaven had to pass through Purgatory first. This was half-way between Heaven and Hell. As you passed through, you were punished to clean you from your sins. But the Church provided help for you to get out of Purgatory more quickly.

During your life you could buy 'indulgences' from a bishop, which meant you weren't punished for sins. In fact, any money given to the Church for the building, decoration or repair of your parish church could help you in Purgatory.

SOURCE 2 A fifteenth-century stained-glass window at Doddiscombsleigh Church in Devon. It shows a Mass, a baptism, a marriage and the last rites

You could also get out of Purgatory more quickly if you had masses said for your soul. So rich people left money in their wills to build 'chantry' chapels where priests said masses for their souls.

The Mass (Source 2) was said daily by the priest. Most people believed that at the Mass the bread and wine actually became the body and blood of Christ. The priest was 'sacrificing' Christ each time the Mass was said. This made the priest special.

How far did people still believe in all this in 1500? Look at Sources 3–7 to find out.

SOURCE 3 A description by an Italian visitor to England in 1497

> *People always hear Mass on Sunday and give generously to the Church and the poor.*
>
> *There is not a parish church in the kingdom that does not have crucifixes, candlesticks and cups of silver, as well as many other ornaments worthy of a cathedral.*

SOURCE 1 Inside a typical medieval Roman Catholic church in 1500

Labels in Source 1: Rood screen, Mass book, Chalice, Altar, Server, Priest, Rushes on floor

SOURCE 4 The will of Richard Berne, London, 1525

My body is to be buried in the place near the chapel that I caused to be made in the south aisle of St Magnus' Church.

For tithes forgotten: 3s 4d.

For masses to be said in the church for my soul, my wife's soul and all Christian souls, every month for one year after my death: £6.

Every Friday for a year after my death 3s 4d to be given to prisoners in Newgate one Friday, those in Ludgate the next Friday.

The very best canvas for shirts and smocks for the poor people in Bedfordshire.

£100 towards the making of an altar table.

SOURCE 5 A description by Roger Martin of what Melford Church looked like in the 1520s

At the back of the high altar a carving of Christ's crucifixion.

At the north end of the same altar a large gilt image of the Holy Trinity.

In my chapel at the back of the altar a table with a crucifix on it, with the two thieves hanging.

To the north of the altar from the ground to the roof a painting of Jesus, and to the south a painting of the Blessed Lady.

A rood-loft, with the rood [a crucifix] and Mary and John. The loft going right across the church. On its side, painted, the twelve disciples.

All the roof beautified with gilt stars.

In the vestry many rich copes and vestments.

In the choir, in a recess in the north wall, the sepulchre [the 'tomb' where the leftover bread and wine from Mass were brought].

SOURCE 7 From a list of church goods in Melford in 1529

A chalice, the gift of Mawt Barker, gilt, 21 ounces.
A chalice, the gift of John Hill, gilt, 20 ounces.
A relic of the pillar that Christ was bound to, the gift of Sir William Clopton.
A silver pot, the gift of Mother Barrel.
Two silver candlesticks, the gift of old John Smith, 61 ounces.
Total of 80 ornaments, rings and crucifixes.
An altar cloth of silk with blue birds, bordered with blue velvet.
Total of 20 copes and vestments.
A Mass book, the gift of John Hill.

1. On your own copy of the plan in Source 6, try to mark the items mentioned in Source 5 in the right places. Also label each of the altars.
2. Look at Sources 4 and 7. Why did people give so much to the Church and to the poor?

Activity

It is 1500. You are a government official sent out to report on whether people are still supporting the Catholic Church and accepting its beliefs. Using the evidence about church buildings and people's wills on this page, write a report explaining your findings so far.

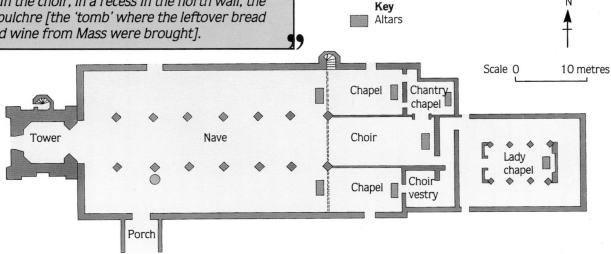

Key
Altars

N

Scale 0   10 metres

Tower   Nave   Chapel   Chantry chapel
         Choir
         Chapel   Choir vestry   Lady chapel
Porch

SOURCE 6 Plan of Melford Church

Henry VIII: Catholic or Protestant?

MOST evidence suggests that in the early sixteenth century ordinary people were still quite happy with the Church. They did not mind that services and churches had not changed much since the Middle Ages. But in the 1500s this situation changed.

People began to criticise the Church. They said it was too wealthy and did not use its money to help the poor. Instead, the bishops and the monks in MONASTERIES lived in luxury.

Many priests and bishops had several jobs. This meant they couldn't do them all properly. Some priests never visited their parishes, leaving people who could not read or write to take the services.

The services and the Bible were still in Latin. Many people said they found it difficult to feel close to God if they couldn't read the Bible for themselves or understand the services.

In England, a group called the Lollards had been making these criticisms for years. Then in 1519 in Germany a monk called Luther attacked the Catholic Church. He was especially angry about the idea of paying to have your sins forgiven (indulgences). Soon many people joined Luther in protesting against these things. They were called 'Protestants'. The changes and reforms the Protestants brought about in churches all over Europe are known as the Reformation.

Henry VIII

When King Henry VIII of England first heard of Luther's ideas he wrote a book defending the Catholic Church. Yet by 1536 he had declared himself, rather than the Pope, to be head of the English Church, and had closed down all the monasteries in England.

Do these events show that Henry was a Protestant, or did he have other reasons for these actions?

---

1. Look at Sources 1–3. Which of Henry's actions seem to support the Protestants?
2. Which seem to support the Catholics?

▶ **SOURCE 1** Engraving showing the punishment of monks in 1535. They had stood up to Henry and refused to recognise him as Head of the Church

SOURCE 2 Religious policies of Henry VIII

66 *1532–3 Acts passed which stopped all payments to the Pope from the English Church.*
1534 Act of Supremacy made the king head of the English Church instead of the Pope.
1536 Smaller monasteries dissolved (closed down).
1538 Henry's son Edward born. Although he knew Edward would be the next king, Henry decided to have him educated by two leading Protestants.
1539 Larger monasteries dissolved.
1539 English translation of the Bible published.
1539 Act of Six Articles supported all Catholic beliefs and Catholic church services; said Protestants were to be persecuted.

SOURCE 3 The execution of William Tyndale in 1536. He was persecuted by Henry, and later executed by the Holy Roman Emperor for translating the Bible into English so that ordinary people could read it

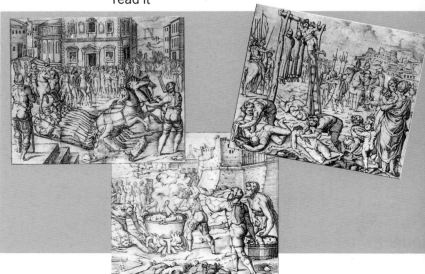

If we are going to understand these confusing actions, we need to know a little more about Henry's problems.

Henry wanted a son. His wife, ...erine of Aragon, had given him a ...ghter, Mary, but no son. Catherine had ...several miscarriages and it was clear ...the chances of her giving birth to a ...thy son were small. Henry believed that ...make sure the TUDOR dynasty survived ...needed a son.

...By 1525 Henry had decided that he ...nted a new wife to give him a son. Only ...e Pope could give Henry a divorce and the ...ope refused.

Meanwhile, Henry had fallen in love with ...nne Boleyn. At the end of 1532 she was ...regnant with Henry's child. In 1533 ...ranmer, Archbishop of Canterbury, acted ...n orders from Henry and declared Anne ...nd Henry man and wife.

■ **Henry was bankrupt.** He wanted to be powerful in Europe. He had already fought some very expensive wars in Europe and now desperately needed more money. The monasteries were very rich. They owned about a quarter of all the land in the country. If Henry took over the monasteries he would be very rich.

■ **Henry wanted to control the Church.** Since medieval times there had been repeated struggles over whether the priests and Church leaders should obey the Pope or the king. (You will remember the battle between Archbishop Becket and King Henry II that led to Becket's murder.) The powerful monasteries were loyal to the Pope. Henry VIII resented an outsider being in control of so big a part of English life. He wanted to control the Church in his own country.

3. Look back at Sources 1–3. Which of these statements do you most agree with now?
■ 'Henry couldn't decide if he supported the Catholics or the Protestants.'
■ 'Henry supported whoever would help him get what he wanted.'
■ 'Henry generally supported the Catholics, but went along with Protestant ideas when they could get him what he wanted.'

Why did Henry close the monasteries?

Most of the monasteries and nunneries in England were supposed to follow strict rules, laid down by Saint Benedict 900 years earlier. These showed how monks and nuns were meant to live. The rules made sure they devoted their lives to God and to helping other people.

Activity

Look at Source 1. Write an article for a Catholic newspaper in 1535, describing in no more than 60 words what is happening to the monks.
Then invent the best headline for the article that you can think of.

SOURCE 4 The rules for monks and nuns

❝ *They should:*
■ *live as poor people*
■ *not marry or have sexual relationships*
■ *look after the poor, the sick and the old*
■ *give shelter and food to travellers*
■ *eat simply and fast regularly. Their main meal at two o'clock should be fish, vegetables and bread. No meat was allowed*
■ *wear simple, rough clothes*
■ *sleep in dormitories with the other monks or nuns. Have just a mattress, blanket and pillow on their bed*
■ *help to educate children*
■ *copy out precious or rare manuscripts.* ❞

HENRY VIII: CATHOLIC OR PROTESTANT?

In 1535 Thomas Cromwell, Henry's chief minister, sent out handpicked inspectors to report on the state of the monasteries. He was looking for excuses to close them down. The inspectors were given a list of questions. They then wrote reports back to Cromwell. Some reports which praised the monasteries were sent back to the inspectors by Cromwell with instructions to be more critical.

1. Look at Source 5. What examples are there of monks not living as they should?
2. What was the most common crime reported?
3. What evidence is there that the inspectors were deliberately trying to find something wrong?
4. Does the evidence in Source 5 prove that the monasteries were corrupt and should be closed down?

SOURCE 5 Extracts from some of the reports Cromwell received
a) About Crossed Friars monastery, London

Found the prior at that time in bed with a woman, both naked, about 11 o'clock in the morning.

b) About an abbey near Chichester

The Abbey of Essebourne and the Priory of Shulbred, because of their poverty, were not able to lodge us. We were compelled to ride out of our way to Waverley Abbey to lodge.

c) About Langdon in Kent

I spent a good time knocking at the abbot's door, neither sound nor sign of life appearing. I found a short pole-axe standing behind the door, and with it I dashed the door to pieces. About the house I go, and find his woman.

d) About Woolsthorpe in Lincolnshire

I write to you in support of the house of Woolstrope. The abbot is well beloved, having eight religious persons, being priests of right good conversation and living religiously, having such qualities of virtue as we have not found the like in any place.

e) About St Edmund's monastery, in Suffolk

The Abbot delighted much in playing at dice and in that spent much money. For his own pleasure he has had lots of beautiful buildings built.

f) About the St Edmund's convent

I could not find out anything bad about the convent, no matter how hard I tried. I believe I couldn't find anything because everybody had got together and agreed to keep the convent's secrets ... Among the relics we found were enough pieces of the Holy Cross to make a whole cross.

The inspectors did not visit all the monasteries they reported on. Instead of a personal visit they often just asked people living close by to tell them what the monastery was like.

Most monasteries had also been regularly visited by their local bishop. The bishops usually came to different judgements to the inspectors'. For example, at Shulbrede in Sussex Cromwell's inspectors reported that the prior had seven mistresses. The bishop, on the other hand, said all was well.

SOURCE 6 Robert Aske explains why he and thousands of others in northern England rebelled against Henry in 1536

The closing of the monasteries means that religious services will not be carried out, and the poor will not be looked after. The monasteries are much loved by the people.

SOURCE 7 By a modern historian

Henry's normal income before 1536 was about £100,000 a year. Between 1536 and 1547 he received an extra £140,000 a year from the dissolution of the monasteries.

5. Does the new evidence you have just read show why it is important for historians to look at as much evidence as possible?

In 1536 the small monasteries were dissolved (closed down). In 1539 all the big monasteries were also dissolved. Not one monastery was left in England. The King took much of the land and the valuables. Other land was sold to the nobles and GENTRY. Some abbey buildings fell into ruin, some became private houses while a few became cathedrals.

6. Do you think Henry VIII closed the monasteries:
- because they were so corrupt
- because he needed money
- for other reasons?

Explain your answer by referring to the evidence on pages 28–30.

SOURCE 8 Fountains Abbey, which fell into ruins after it was sold off by Henry VIII

Edward VI

When Henry died in 1547, his only surviving son Edward became king at the age of nine. He had been educated as a Protestant. Edward's Protestant advisers influenced him to change official policies on religion. Real changes in the services and beliefs of the Church began to take place.

SOURCE 9 Religious policies of Edward VI

1547 Chantries were dissolved – this was an attack on the belief in Purgatory and the practice of saying prayers for the dead.
1549 Priests were allowed to get married. The Catholic church did not allow priests to marry.
1552 A new Protestant Prayer Book was introduced for the Church, with services in English, not Latin. Remember that the Prayer Book laid down all the beliefs of the Church.

SOURCE 10 Changes in the new Prayer Book

- *The Mass was abolished and replaced with the communion service. At communion the bread and the wine only represented Christ, they did not become Christ. It was a service of remembrance, not a sacrifice.*
- *Altars were replaced by simple tables.*
- *Priests no longer wore the elaborate vestments popular in Catholic churches.*
- *Finally, the idea of Predestination was accepted. This was the belief that it had already been decided whether a person was going to Heaven or Hell. You could not buy your way to heaven by good works or prayers for your soul.*

Activity

Look at Sources 9–11. Make a list of all the changes made to the Church during Edward's reign. Then make a list of all the changes made to the Church by Henry.

Who do you think changed the Church more?

Prayer book

Pulpit for preaching

Bread for Communion   Wine for Communion

Tiled floor

SOURCE 11 A church in Edward's reign

Bloody Queen Mary?

IN 1553 Edward VI died. His sister Mary became queen. She was a devout Catholic, who believed that unless the Roman Catholic Church was brought back no one in England would be able to go to Heaven.

Was it possible to bring Catholicism back? Read through this list of factors which would affect whether Mary could succeed:

- Protestantism had only been the official religion of England for six years. Before that, England had been a Catholic country for centuries. Many people would be glad to go back to familiar Catholic ideas.
- Henry VIII had already closed all the monasteries and sold their lands to rich and important people. Mary would have to take all this land back.
- There were many Protestants in England. They hated the Pope and Catholicism.
- Mary was 37, was not married and had no children. Her sister Elizabeth was next in line to the throne. She was a Protestant.
- Four hundred of the most important Protestant leaders fled to Europe in 1553.
- When Mary became queen, Protestants had tried to replace her. They received no support.

---

1. Which of these points suggest that Mary had a good chance of bringing back Catholicism?
2. Which suggest that Mary did not stand much chance of bringing back Catholicism?
3. On balance, how good do you think Mary's chances were?

Once Mary had decided to bring back Catholicism she had to decide how to do it. She could:
- reform and improve the Catholic Church so that many people would want to be Catholics again
- get the support of a powerful Catholic country. Spain was the most powerful Catholic country in Europe
- force people to become Catholics by persecuting Protestants.

---

4. Which methods would you recommend Mary to use?

Mary's methods

In 1554 Mary married the Catholic King Philip II of Spain. This provoked a rebellion in Kent. The rebels almost captured London, but were eventually defeated.

Between 1555 and 1558 Mary had 284 Protestants burned to death. She was hoping that this would persuade other Protestants to return to Catholicism.

SOURCE 1 Simon Renard, a Catholic, was the Spanish Ambassador in London. He wrote this letter to King Philip after watching the first Protestant being burnt at the stake in 1555

" *A certain Rogers was burned publicly yesterday. Some of the onlookers wept, others prayed to God to give him strength to bear the pain, others gathered the ashes and the bones and wrapped them in paper to preserve them, others threatened the bishops. I think it would be wise not to be too firm against Protestants, otherwise I foresee that the people may cause a revolt. The lady Elizabeth has her supporters, and there are Englishmen who do not love foreigners.*

SOURCE 2 The execution of Latimer and Ridley, tw Protestant bishops who refused to become Catholic

SOURCE 3 From John Foxe's *Book of Martyrs*, about the burning of Latimer and Ridley

So they came to the stake. Dr Ridley, entering the place first, looked towards Heaven. Then, seeing Mr Latimer, with a cheerful look he ran and embraced him, saying, 'Be of good heart, brother, for God will either ease the fury of the flame, or else strengthen us to endure it.'

He then went to the stake and, kneeling down, prayed with great fervour, while Mr Latimer following, kneeled down and prayed also. Dr Ridley gave presents of small things to men standing near, many of whom were weeping strongly. Happy was he who could get the smallest rag to remember this good man by. Then the blacksmith took a chain of iron and placed it about both their waists and then knocked in the staple.

Dr Ridley's brother brought him a bag of gunpowder and tied it about his neck. His brother did the same to Mr Latimer.

They then brought a lighted faggot and laid it at Dr Ridley's feet. Upon which Mr Latimer said, 'Be of good comfort, Mr Ridley, we shall this day light such a candle, by God's grace, in England, as I trust never shall be put out.'

Mr Latimer cried out, 'Father of Heaven, receive my soul', and soon died with seeming little pain. But Dr Ridley, due to the bad arrangement of the fire (the faggots being green and piled so high, that the flames were kept down by the green wood), laboured in much pain until one of the bystanders pulled the faggots with a hook. Where Ridley saw the fire flame up, he leaned himself to that side. As soon as the fire touched the gunpowder he was seen to stir no more. The dreadful sight filled almost every eye with tears.

1. What evidence can you find in Source 3 that the author was a Protestant?
2. Do you think that Source 2 shows the same event as that described in Source 3?
3. Do you think it is from the same book as Source 3?
4. Look back at the three possible methods for bringing back Catholicism. Which of the three methods described did Mary use? Which did she not use?

Bloody Mary?

During her reign many people thought Mary was succeeding in bringing back Catholicism. However, the way we see Mary's reign today has been influenced by Foxe's *Book of Martyrs*. This was published by a Protestant in Elizabeth's reign. It treats the people burned as heroes and tells us that the executions were unpopular. It assumes that everyone was against Mary. Above all else, it makes Mary out to be 'Bloody Mary'. Is any of this true?

To answer the question we need to try to look at the events as seen during Mary's reign — not after.

We must be careful not to judge people in the past by our standards today. In the sixteenth century people were used to HERETICS being burned:
- Henry VII burned ten in 24 years
- Henry VIII burned 81 in 38 years
- Edward VI burned two in six years
- Mary burned 284 in five years
- Elizabeth burned five in 45 years.

If we look only at these facts, we might think Mary deserved her nickname. However, if we look at other facts about executions under the Tudors we might change our minds.

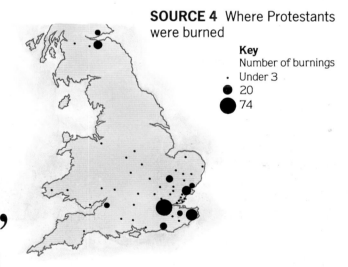

SOURCE 4 Where Protestants were burned

Key
Number of burnings
· Under 3
● 20
⬤ 74

- Every year between 17 and 54 people were hanged in Essex for small-scale theft.
- After the Northern Rebellion in Elizabeth's reign over 300 people were hanged.

1. Look at Source 4. Do you think people all around the country would have thought that Mary was 'Bloody Mary'? Explain why.
2. Do you agree with Foxe that Mary deserves to be called 'Bloody Mary'?

The Reformation in English villages

MARY died in November 1558, still only 42 years old. She had not had a child. And she had not had enough time to make everyone Catholic.

Most people were relieved when Mary's sister Elizabeth became queen in 1558. Mary had turned many people against Catholicism, because they now associated it with cruel persecution.

Elizabeth would probably have brought back Protestantism in any case, but she had little choice — nearly everybody wanted to see the end of Catholicism.

In 1559 Elizabeth was made head of the Church of England. The Prayer Book of Edward's reign was brought back. Protestants were very keen on people reading the Bible for themselves and clergy using it for sermons, so a Bible in English was made available in every church. Priests were allowed to marry again.

From then on, England remained officially Protestant.

The Reformation in Melford Church

So far we have been looking at the changes made by kings, queens and Parliament. What about the village churches and the ordinary people? How were they affected? Had they all become Protestant by 1558?

To investigate this we are going to return first to Melford Church in Suffolk, which we looked at on page 27.

If we look at the church accounts during Edward's reign, we find that the churchwardens were selling off the contents of the church (see Source 2).

SOURCE 2 From Melford Church accounts, 1547–1548

Sold to Master Clopton the biggest images in the church for 3s.
Sold to Mr Clopton the altar in Our Lady Chapel for 6s 8d.
Sold 300lb of wax for £2 10s.
Sold to John Dowty some wood and half a crucifix for 8d.

At the same time the church was spending money to have various jobs done.

SOURCE 3 Melford Church accounts, 1547–1548

7s 1d paid to Rafe Borom and his lad and Robert Alefounder and his lad for taking down the images.
1s 2d paid for the taking down of the font and the high altar.
£1 14s 8d paid to John Kendall for the whitewashing of the church.
10s paid to Rafe Borom for taking down the rood loft.

If we then move to the accounts for Mary's reign, we find rather different changes taking place.

SOURCE 4 From Melford Church accounts, 1554–1556

6s 8d paid to a painter of Sudbury for the painting of the high altar.
1s paid to the carpenter for the making of the sepulchre.
7d paid to Sponer for the making of surplices.
3s paid for scrubbing out the scribbling on the church walls.
9s 10d paid for the making of the rood.
10s paid to Lyghtman for painting and gilding the rood.

Finally, in Elizabeth's reign, we find the church having to reverse everything again, although some of the work was not being done until five years after Elizabeth became queen, and some not until the 1570s (see Source 5).

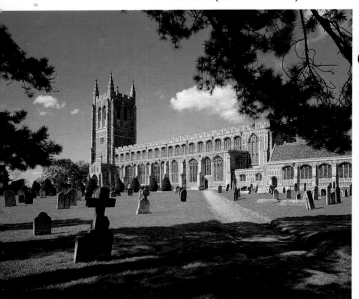

SOURCE 1 Melford Church

1548 Edward's reign

1555 Mary's reign

1562 Elizabeth's reign

SOURCE 5 From Melford Church accounts

"*1562* 15s received from Symond Causon for the timber that was on the rood loft.
1562 10s 8d received from Gylles Gringras for 4 boards that belonged to the altar.
1572 £6 15s 6d received for a chalice.
1575 10s received for vestments
1577 2s paid to Fyrmyn the glazier for defacing the images in the glass windows."

Around the country

Were other areas of the country quicker or slower than Melford to accept the changes?

■ A survey in 1562 showed that half the churches of Lincoln still had not got rid of their altars.
■ In Sussex in 1569 it was reported that there were 'images and other popish [Catholic] objects, hidden ready to set the Mass up again'.

SOURCE 6 Reports from Weaverham in Cheshire

"*1578* They lack a Communion Book and a Bible. There is in the church an altar standing defaced. The people will not be stopped from ringing the bells on All Saints' Day. They refuse to take communion with usual bread. Crosses are standing in the churchyard.
1589 The villagers weep and bewail seeing the bare walls, and lacking their images and chalices."

1. Make a timeline from 1545 to 1580. Mark on it the changes made at Melford described in Sources 2–5. Show which changes made the church more Catholic, and which made it more Protestant.
2. In a class discussion, decide which of these words best describe the religious changes in English villages: immediate, gradual, local, national, short-term, long-term.

Activity

It is 1590. You are a priest. You were the priest of Melford during the reigns of Henry, Edward, Mary and Elizabeth. You are now priest of Weaverham. You still support Catholic beliefs.

Write a letter to an old friend in Melford describing the changes that have taken place in the English Church and how you feel about them. Which have affected you most?

Were the Catholics framed?

READ Source 1. It is from a book written for children in 1835. It tells you what children at that time were taught about the Gunpowder Plot of 1605. Most people today still believe this story.

Christopher Wright

John Wright

Robert Winter

Bates

Thom Perc

SOURCE 1 From *Little Arthur's History of England* by Lady Callcott, 1835

"*King James I dealt severely with the Catholics, whom he put in prison and from whom he took a lot of money. The Catholics grew tired of this. Some of them thought that if they could kill him they might have a Catholic king or queen.*

From thinking wickedly they went on to do wickedly. They found that there were some cellars under the Houses of Parliament, and they filled these cellars with gunpowder; and as they expected the Parliament and the King to meet there on 5 November they hired a man called Guy Fawkes to set fire to the gunpowder, and so to blow it up and kill everybody there.

Now, it happened that one of the lords, whose name was Mounteagle, had a friend among the Catholics, and that friend wrote him a letter, without signing his name, to beg him not to go to the Parliament that day because a sudden blow would be struck which would destroy them all. Lord Mounteagle took this letter to the king's council. Some of the councillors laughed at it. But the King thought about it and said the sudden blow must mean gunpowder. He set people to watch the vaults under the Parliament, till at last they caught Guy Fawkes with his lantern, waiting for the time to set fire to the gunpowder."

1. How can you tell that this account was written for children?
2. Whose side do you think the author was on, the Catholics' or the King's? What clues helped you to your answer?

▲ **SOURCE 2** The Gunpowder Plotters – an engraving made soo after the plot by a Dutch artist wh probably never saw them

3. Choose one word which best sums up the impression Source 2 gives of the plotters.
4. Look at Source 4. Has the artist got it right? Draw a more accurate version.

Some people do not accept this story. Some Catholics at the time and historians today argue that Robert Cecil – a Protestant – who was King James' chief minister, planned the whole thing. He wanted to discredit the Catholics and force James to punish them severely. They say that one of the supposed plotters, Francis Tresham, was actually working for Cecil and that it was Tresham who sent the anonymous letter to Mounteagle.

See what you think from the following evidence.

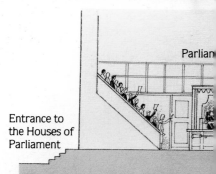

Parlian

Entrance to the Houses of Parliament

SOURCE 3 Artist's impression of the plotters at work

Guido Fawkes   Robert Catesby   Thomas Winter

SOURCE 5 An extract from the letter sent to Lord Mounteagle. The letter was delivered to him by a disguised messenger at his London house on 26 October. This was the only night in 1605 that Lord Mounteagle stayed in his London house

My lord, I have a care for your safety. Therefore I would advise you to devise some excuse to miss your attendance at this Parliament. For God and man have come together to punish the wickedness of this time. Go into the country, for they shall receive a terrible blow this Parliament – and yet they shall not see who hurts them.

5. Why do you think the messenger was in disguise?
6. Who do you think sent the letter?

SOURCE 6 King James' orders about Guy Fawkes' interrogation after he was arrested

If he will not otherwise confess, the gentler tortures are to be first used, and then the uttermost pain.

SOURCE 7 From Guy Fawkes' confession

He said he did not intend to set fire to the fuse until the King came into the Houses of Parliament, and then he intended to do it so that the powder might blow up a quarter of an hour later.

SOURCE 4 The Venetian Ambassador's account of a conversation he had with Robert Cecil. The Venetian Ambassador was a Catholic. According to the Ambassador this is what Cecil said

The King's excessive kindness has ended in this, that Catholic priests go openly about the country saying Mass. This gives great offence to others. We cannot hope for good government while we have a large number of people who obey foreign rulers as the Catholics do. The priests preach that Catholics must even kill the King to help their religion.

Guido Fawkes
G. Guido

SOURCE 8 Guy Fawkes' normal signature, alongside his signature to his confession

7. Can you suggest reasons why Guy Fawkes' signature to his confession is so different from his normal signature?
8. Does this mean that Guy Fawkes' confession cannot be trusted?

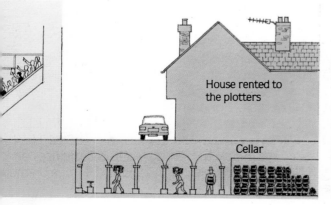

House rented to the plotters

Cellar

WERE THE CATHOLICS FRAMED?

SOURCE 9 An extract from Thomas Winter's confession. We do not know whether the confession is genuine. Cecil never showed the original confession to the court – he had a new copy written out for the trial

We were working under a little entry to the Parliament house. We under-propped it with wood. We bought the gunpowder and hid it in Mr Percy's house. We worked another two weeks against the stone wall, which was very hard to get through. At that time we called in Kit Wright.

About Easter we rented the cellar. After this Mr Fawkes laid into the cellar 1000 sticks and 500 faggots.

---

1. Which men in Source 2 does Winter's confession incriminate?

SOURCE 10 Some important facts to consider

■ *At that time all gunpowder was controlled by the government. All supplies were kept in the Tower of London.*

■ *The 36 barrels of gunpowder were placed in the cellar of a house next to Parliament. The cellar ran under the Houses of Parliament. This cellar was rented to the plotters by John Whynniard, a king's official and a friend of Cecil.*

■ *Lord Mounteagle told the King about the plot on 27 October and yet the government took no action until 4 November.*

■ *The government seemed to know where all the plotters were. On 7 November they were surrounded in Holbeach House. They offered no resistance and yet some of them were shot dead.*

■ *All the plotters were killed or captured quickly, except one, Francis Tresham. He was left free until 12 December. Once the trial of the other plotters was over he was taken prisoner and died of a mysterious illness in the Tower of London on 23 December.*

SOURCE 11 Written by an Italian (Catholic) visitor in 1605

Some hold it as certain that there has been foul play and that some of the government secretly spun a web to entangle these poor gentlemen.

SOURCE 12 A print from the time showing the execution of the plotters. After their trial for treason they were hung, drawn and quartered

---

2. Does Source 12 prove that Catholics were hated and feared by most people in England?

Cecil must have been very pleased with the way events turned out after the plot. The Catholics became very unpopular. Harsher laws were passed against them. For example, Catholics could not become doctors, lawyers or government officials.

James wanted the plot to be remembered. He asked the people to light their autumn bonfires on 5 November. People put models of the Pope on their fires and burned them.

3. The confessions of Guy Fawkes and Thomas Winter (Sources 7 and 9) say nothing about Cecil setting up the plot. Does this prove that Cecil did not plan it?
4. What does each of the points in Source 10 suggest about who might have planned the plot?
5. Is there enough evidence in Sources 10 and 11 to cast doubts on the usual story, as told in Source 1? Explain your answer.

Activity

Work in pairs. One of you has to organise the prosecution case against the plotters, and one of you has to plan the defence case. Make two lists:

■ which witnesses you want to question
■ what questions you will ask them (remember that they might not all be telling the truth).

Write your closing speech to convince the jury that you are right.

What did Elizabeth look like?

SOURCE 1

SOURCE 2

SOURCE 3

SOURCES 1, 2 and 3 all show Queen Elizabeth. One of them was painted when she was twelve years old. No one expected then that she would become queen. The other two were painted at the beginning of her reign (when she was in her twenties) and at the end of her reign (when she was in her sixties). Can you decide which picture is which? Your teacher can tell you whether you are right.

Elizabeth became queen in 1558. After the divisions of Mary's reign, Elizabeth had to win the loyalty of her people — Catholics and Protestants alike. She had to convince them that she was the right person to be ruler of England.

Equally important, she had to convince the doubters who thought a woman could not govern a country by herself.

---

1. Which of the following words do you think Elizabeth would want people to associate with her: powerful, cruel, good, weak, beautiful, young?
2. Make a list of methods a politician can use today to win people's loyalty. Could Elizabeth have used any of these methods?

One of the best ways for Elizabeth to win people's loyalty was to tour the country, and let people see her. But Elizabeth had a problem. Many parts of the country were too remote and too hostile to a Protestant queen for her to risk travelling there. So instead, Elizabeth used portraits and pictures to let people see her.

Elizabeth wanted to create an image of herself which would impress her subjects. This meant that paintings of the Queen had to be controlled. It would be no good if paintings of Elizabeth showed her to be ugly, old and weak.

In 1563, and at intervals throughout her reign, the government issued portraits of the Queen. These were to be copied by all artists. No other portraits of the Queen were allowed. Masks of Elizabeth's face were also issued. On the whole, this policy seems to have worked. Artists were still copying these 'official' pictures years later. Even miniatures — to be worn round an admirer's neck — copied the official portraits.

Portraits, however, would only have been seen by a few people. They would be hung in the houses of the rich and powerful to show their loyalty to Elizabeth. The government also needed to control other pictures of Elizabeth that everyone would see.

---

3. Look at Sources 1–8. Match them up with captions A–H in the box.
4. Which of these sources would be seen by most people? Give your reasons.
5. Which picture would Elizabeth be most pleased with?
6. Choose one of Sources 1–8 which you think is most reliable in showing what Elizabeth really looked like. Explain your choice.
7. Compare Sources 4 and 8. Did the view of Elizabeth's reign change after her death?

SOURCE 4

SOURCE 7

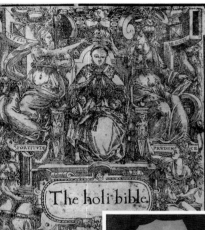

SOURCE 5

SOURCE 8

SOURCE 6

Captions

A Painted when she was twelve years old and no one expected she would become queen

B Painted at the end of her reign when she was in her sixties

C Painted shortly after Elizabeth's death, when people were quite relieved she had died and were glad that a new monarch was on the throne. It shows her looking old and weary

D Painted twenty years after her death, when many people were looking back to 'The Golden Age of Elizabeth'. Elizabeth is seen as St George killing off Catholicism

E Painted at the beginning of her reign when she was about 25 years old

F Painted in 1588, shortly after the Spanish Armada was defeated. The Armada is shown sailing towards England and being wrecked off the Scottish coast. Elizabeth's hand is on a globe to show that she is Empress of the world

G A picture from the front of the English Bible. There was a Bible in every church and many people had their own Bibles

H A miniature of Elizabeth. This would be worn around the neck in a locket, or in a ring

---

8. Check whether each of these statements is right or wrong. Your teacher will discuss your answers with you.
- Elizabeth became queen in 1558.
- Elizabeth was ugly.
- Elizabeth was the daughter of Henry VIII.
- Elizabeth was a better queen than Mary.
- The Spanish Armada tried to invade England in 1601.

Activity

You are a member of Elizabeth's government. You are in control of portraits. Decide which three portraits on this page you want people to copy. You will need to explain which groups in society you are trying to get your message across to, and explain what message about Elizabeth you are trying to get across.

Why did civil war break out in 1642?

ON 22 AUGUST 1642 King Charles I declared war against his enemies in Parliament. In the Civil War which followed one man in ten was killed. Many people died of starvation. Others had their house, their land or all their possessions destroyed.

How had the situation come about where Englishmen were prepared to fight against each other, and even against members of their own families?

The timeline on this page shows you some of the important events which led to the Civil War. But it is rather misleading, because when events are laid out like this it makes the war look inevitable.

This is not how people saw the events at the time. The majority of people in England – even those most closely involved in the events that led to it – had no idea a civil war was on its way until it had started.

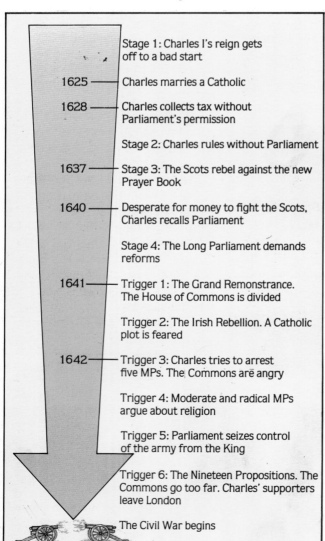

Stage 1: Charles I's reign gets off to a bad start

1625 — Charles marries a Catholic

1628 — Charles collects tax without Parliament's permission

Stage 2: Charles rules without Parliament

1637 — Stage 3: The Scots rebel against the new Prayer Book

1640 — Desperate for money to fight the Scots, Charles recalls Parliament

Stage 4: The Long Parliament demands reforms

1641 — Trigger 1: The Grand Remonstrance. The House of Commons is divided

Trigger 2: The Irish Rebellion. A Catholic plot is feared

1642 — Trigger 3: Charles tries to arrest five MPs. The Commons are angry

Trigger 4: Moderate and radical MPs argue about religion

Trigger 5: Parliament seizes control of the army from the King

Trigger 6: The Nineteen Propositions. The Commons go too far. Charles' supporters leave London

The Civil War begins

The background: King and Parliament

By the seventeenth century the King of England could no longer rule the country by himself. He needed Parliament to help him.

Parliament contained the most powerful people in the country. In the House of Lords there were the nobles and bishops. In the House of Commons there were elected MPs, who were mostly rich landowners but also included a few rich merchants.

New laws had to be passed by both Parliament and the king, so the king needed Parliament on his side.

If the king needed money for emergencies, such as wars, he had to ask Parliament to vote him a tax which people all around the country would have to pay. When the king asked Parliament for a tax it had a chance to demand that he took some notice of its ideas. So during the sixteenth century the power of Parliament had gradually been growing.

Stage 1:

Charles I's reign gets off to a bad start

Charles I's reign got off to a very bad start.

■ In 1625 Charles married a French Catholic princess, Henrietta Maria. This was very unpopular with Parliament.

■ Parliament also distrusted Charles' main adviser, Buckingham (see Source 1). In 1626 Parliament tried to punish him for bungling a naval expedition against Spain. Charles sent two MPs to prison because of this.

> **SOURCE 1** A popular rhyme at the beginning of Charles' reign
>
> 66 *Who rules the country? The King.*
> *Who rules the King? The Duke [Buckingham].*
> *Who rules the Duke? The Devil.*

■ Then there was the question of money. When a new king or queen came to the throne Parliament usually voted to give the monarch the income from customs duties for life. When Charles became king Parliament voted to grant him the customs duties for only one year. They were trying to force him to call Parliament regularly. But Charles carried on collecting the duties anyway, without Parliament's permission.

Stage 2:

Charles rules without Parliament

In 1629 Charles I dissolved Parliament. He then ruled without Parliament for eleven years, until 1640. Some historians say that his policies in this period – particularly his taxes and his religious reforms – were very unpopular and brought civil war very close. Other historians say that England was well ruled during this period and that most people were very happy.

See what you think.

Money

Now that Charles did not have a Parliament he had to find new ways to raise money.

One method he used was 'Ship Money'. This was a tax that was usually used to improve the navy in times of war. And usually it was paid only by counties on the coast. In 1634 Charles asked the coastal counties for Ship Money even though England was not at war and had no need to improve the navy. The following year, 1635, Ship Money was demanded from the inland counties as well. It looked as if Charles meant the tax to be permanent, paid every year.

One way of finding out if a tax is unpopular is to see whether people paid it or not.

I refuse to pay Ship Money unless the King recalls Parliament to approve the tax.

This court upholds the King's right to raise this tax without Parliament's permission. You must pay!

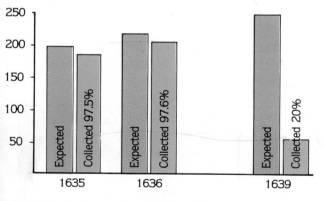

SOURCE 2 Some details of the Ship Money tax, 1635–9

(bar chart: 1635 — Expected ~200, Collected 97.5% ~185; 1636 — Expected ~215, Collected 97.6% ~205; 1639 — Expected ~245, Collected 20% ~50)

SOURCE 4 When the tax was extended to inland counties a man called John Hampden refused to pay. He said Parliament should be asked to agree to the tax first. The judges decided the King was right

SOURCE 5 From a recent history book

> *Ship Money was a financial success. But the political cost was immense. Charles offended every class in the country – the lords, the gentry and the merchants.*

SOURCE 3 Written in October 1637 by a Cambridge don who provided a regular news service for those living abroad

> *All things are calm. There appears no change either in court or affairs. Although taxes are great, people only privately breathe out a little discontent and lay down their purses, for I think the great tax of Ship Money is so well accepted.*

1. What evidence is there to support the following views:
    - 'To start with, Ship Money was accepted by everyone without any fuss. Charles now had more money than he had had for years.'
    - 'Ship Money gradually became more unpopular. By 1639 Charles was in a dangerous situation with most of the country against him.'

Religion

In the 1630s Charles and Archbishop Laud began to make changes to the Church of England. They claimed they were trying to improve it. They believed that people would feel closer to God if churches were decorated and beautiful. They were not very keen on the clergy preaching sermons about the Bible.

These ideas upset a lot of people, particularly the PURITANS. Many thought they were trying to bring the Catholic Church back. Charles' wife was a Catholic and had her own chapel and priest. Perhaps he was also a Catholic!

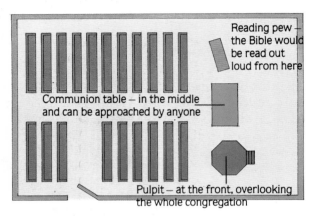

SOURCE 6 A plan of a church in Shropshire, built in 1601

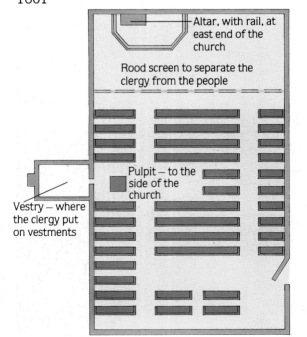

SOURCE 7 A plan of St John's Church in Leeds, built in 1634

> **1.** Which of these churches would a Puritan like? Which would Archbishop Laud like?

Pamphlets began to appear attacking the Church and monarchy (see Source 8).

SOURCE 8 Charles and his advisers are shown cutting down the tree of religion

> **SOURCE 9** In 1637 Archbishop Laud put three Puritans, Prynne, Burton and Bastwick, who had written some of these pamphlets, on trial. They were found guilty and punished severely.
>
> *The executioner cut off Mr Burton's ears, deep and close, in a cruel manner with much bleeding, an artery being cut.*
>
> *Mr Prynne's cheeks were seared with an iron made exceeding hot, after which the executioner cut off one of his ears and a piece of his cheek; then hacking the other ear almost off, left it hanging.*

> **2.** Look at Sources 8 and 10. Were they made by supporters or opponents of Charles' religious policies? Explain your answer.

SOURCE 10 Archbishop Laud eating Puritans' ears for dinner

3. Do you agree with Clarendon's views in Source 11?
4. Why do you think Clarendon wrote this version of the eleven years' rule?

SOURCE 11 Clarendon wrote a *History of the Rebellion* in the 1660s. He was a minister of Charles II (Charles I's son). This is Clarendon's view of these eleven years' rule without Parliament

In this time the kingdom enjoyed the greatest calm and the fullest measure of happiness that any people in any age for so long a time have been blessed with.

England was secure. The country was rich and was enjoying the pleasure of its own wealth. The Protestant religion was advanced against Rome by the writings of the late archbishop [Laud] more than it had been since the Reformation.
"

5. Which do you think was the more important problem — money or religion?
6. Do you think either problem made war inevitable?

Stage 3:
The Scots rebel against the new Prayer Book

Perhaps Charles could have continued to rule without Parliament. But in 1637 he did something which some historians think was a terrible mistake.

Charles was king of both England and Scotland. Scotland was much more Puritan in its religion than England. The Scots had never accepted the English Prayer Book. For them it had always been too close to Catholicism. They rejected any services that looked like Catholic practices and did not even want bishops. But Charles was determined to spread Laud's reforms into Scotland. In 1637 he ordered that the English Prayer Book (which laid down how services should be carried out) should be used in Scotland. He did not ask the Scots about this, he simply told them what to do. Their reaction can be seen in Source 12.

Activity
Write a headline for the events in Source 12. Then write a report explaining what is happening.

SOURCE 12 A seventeenth-century print showing what happened when a clergyman tried to read the new Prayer Book in Scotland

More riots followed. Charles then decided to raise an army to fight the Scots. He made the English pay a tax called 'Coat and Conduct Money' to pay for the army's uniforms, training and transport.

Coming on top of Ship Money it produced a taxpayers' strike in 1639–40. The gentry refused to pay or collect the tax. In Wiltshire soldiers broke open the county gaol to release those imprisoned for not paying Coat and Conduct Money.

Events now moved very quickly. Month by month Charles got deeper and deeper into trouble.

Summer 1639
Strafford Returns!
Strafford, the King's hated minister, has been recalled from Ireland, where he used brutal methods to put down trouble. He has a large army in Ireland. Will he use it in England to force people to do what the King wants?

April 1640
The Short Parliament
Charles calls Parliament, then sends it home after three weeks! Parliament refuses to pay the King more money unless Charles stops the Laud reforms and gets rid of unpopular taxes.

Summer 1640
Scotland – it's war
Charles' army has been defeated in Scotland. The Scots have invaded northern England. And now Charles has agreed to pay the Scots £850 a day until an agreement is reached – money he hasn't got!

November 1640
King desperate for money
Charles has called Parliament again. But Parliament will not give him any money until he drops his unpopular policies and his hated ministers!

> 1. One historian has said: 'Charles' problems were not caused by how he governed in England, but by how he handled Scotland.' Do you agree?

Stage 4:
The Long Parliament demands reform
Charles now appeared to be at the mercy of Parliament. Nearly all the MPs in the House of Commons were united against him.

Yet even now, when Parliament met in November 1640, nobody dreamt that a civil war was close. The possibility was not in anyone's mind. In any case, there was nobody to fight on Charles' side. Almost everyone in Parliament agreed that he had to change his policies, and you need two sides to fight a war.

Sources 13 and 14 contain two lists. Source 13 shows what Parliament demanded from the King when it met in November 1640. Source 14 shows what Charles agreed to by the summer of 1641.

Parliament's demands, November 1640
- Charles' evil ministers must be punished.
- Ministers should be appointed who will advise Charles to follow sensible policies. Some of these ministers should come from Parliament.
- The King must get rid of courts such as the court of the Star Chamber which allow him to lock up his opponents.
- Regular meetings of Parliament must be held.
- There can be no taxes without Parliament's agreement.
- Reverse Laud's reforms of the Church of England.

SOURCE 13 Parliament in 1640

1. Which of Parliament's demands (Source 13) did Charles agree to (Source 14)?
2. Do you agree that by the summer of 1641 Parliament had got most of what it wanted?
3. Which of these statements do you agree with more:
   - 'These demands are revolutionary. They show that Parliament wanted to get rid of the king.'
   - 'These demands show that Parliament was merely trying to get Charles to govern more sensibly.'
4. Was war inevitable by the summer of 1641? Explain your answer.

Concessions by Charles, summer 1641

- Triennial Act has been passed – Parliament must meet at least every three years.
- The Long Parliament cannot be dissolved by Charles without its agreement.
- Strafford has been tried for treason and executed.
- Other ministers (including Laud) are in prison.
- The Tunnage and Poundage Act means Charles can collect customs duties for only two months more.
- The Courts of the Star Chamber and the High Commission have been abolished.
- Ship Money has been made illegal.
- Some of Charles' critics within Parliament have been appointed as Charles' advisers.

SOURCE 14 Charles

Most historians agree that in the summer of 1641 nobody was even thinking civil war was possible. It looked as if the two sides had sorted out most of their differences.

Yet only twelve months later war began. Why? What triggered off the war?

Trigger 1:

November 1641: the Grand Remonstrance

This was a new list of demands made by the House of Commons. The demands included reducing the power of the bishops and that Charles should employ councillors and ministers whom Parliament could trust.

The Grand Remonstrance was narrowly passed by just 159 votes to 148. The Commons was apparently becoming divided. Charles now had some support.

When some MPs called for the Grand Remonstrance to be printed and sold to the public, other MPs became very worried. They didn't want to involve ordinary people in politics.

Trigger 2:

November 1641: the Irish Rebellion

On 1 November news reached London of a rebellion in Ireland. Catholics had risen up against their Protestant rulers. Rumours spread through London like wildfire – 200,000 Protestants had been murdered! Charles was behind the rebellion! It was the first part of a plan to make England Catholic!

SOURCE 15 An English print showing the actions of the Irish rebels

1. Why do you think people in England believed rumours like these?

Trigger 3:

January 1642: Charles tries to arrest five MPs

Many historians think that a civil war was brought closer by Charles himself. MPs did not trust him. They feared he was planning to get rid of Parliament and rule by himself again. In January 1642 Charles did something which convinced MPs that this was what he was planning. Charles burst into the House of Commons with 400 soldiers and demanded that five leading MPs be handed over for arrest.

However, the MPs had been warned and had fled by boat down the Thames. They were then protected by the Council of London and treated like heroes.

SOURCE 17 Written by John Rushworth, a clerk in the House of Commons, from shorthand notes he made at the time

> *The House was informed that His Majesty was coming with a guard of soldiers.*
> *When the King was looking about the House, he asked the Speaker whether any of the five persons were in the House. To which the Speaker, falling on his knee, answered, 'Your Majesty, I have not eyes to see nor tongue to speak in this place'.*

1. Compare Sources 16 and 17. They are supposed to show the same moment in the story. Do they agree about what happened?
2. Which tells you more about what happened?
3. Which source is more reliable?
4. You are a member of the House of Commons. You hear that Charles has left London after his failure to arrest the five MPs. How do you react?

SOURCE 16 The attempted arrest of the five MPs, painted in the nineteenth century

Trigger 4:

February 1642: religious divisions

Whenever Parliament debated the question of religion there were always disagreements.

Some MPs wanted to get rid of Archbishop Laud's reforms. Others wanted to get rid of bishops. Others even wanted to abolish the Church of England.

In February 1642 Parliament voted to throw bishops out of the House of Lords. Moderate MPs became more and more worried and began to think about supporting Charles. They believed that if the bishops and the national church were abolished there would be chaos.

Trigger 5:

March 1642: arguments about the army

England needed an army to put down the Irish rebellion. Who should control it? Kings had always controlled the army in the past, but the King had now left London and in any case MPs did not trust Charles enough to let him have an army which might be used against Parliament. They wanted to control the army themselves. Charles refused. So in March Parliament simply took control of the army without his permission.

Trigger 6:

1 June 1642: the Commons go too far

On 1 June Parliament passed a set of demands called the Nineteen Propositions. This finally divided the King's supporters from his opponents.

SOURCE 18 Some of the Nineteen Propositions

> ■ *All affairs of state, including foreign policy, religion and finance, must be agreed with Parliament.*
> ■ *All ministers must be approved of by Parliament.*
> ■ *Parliament must control the education of the King's children. His children cannot marry without Parliament's approval.*
> ■ *Laws against Catholics must be enforced.*
> ■ *The Church must be reformed as Parliament wants.*
> ■ *Parliament is to control the army.*

---

1. Could Charles have agreed to these demands?
2. Was war now inevitable?

MPs who supported the King felt that the Nineteen Propositions were the last straw. Charles did too. He claimed they would make him a 'mere phantom of a king'. Charles' supporters left London.

In June Parliament ordered each county to organise an army. Charles issued the same order. In many places around the country people were now being forced to make a choice they did not want to make – between King and Parliament.

By August, each side had collected an army. Then on 22 August Charles raised his standard at Nottingham. The Civil War had begun.

---

1. Work in groups. Look through pages 42–49. List as many causes of the Civil War as you can find. You should look for events, decisions or mistakes that led to the worsening relationship between King and Parliament.
2. Put letters next to each one: R if it concerns religion, i.e. the Church or the way people worship; M if it concerns money or taxes; P if it is political, i.e. to do with the actions of King or Parliament. You may have more than one letter on each cause.
3. Which of the stages on the road to war do you think was the most important?
4. Which trigger event in 1641–42 do you think did the most to spark off the war?
5. Who was to blame for the war: Charles or Parliament? Explain your answer.

Activity

Work in pairs. Choose whether your pair is going to be on the King's side or Parliament's side.

It is August 1642. Civil War has been declared and armies have been gathered. You have been asked to prepare a poster or leaflet that will be displayed to all soldiers on your side. It must explain to the soldiers why they are fighting.

Mention whose fault the war is. Explain why your side is fighting. Back up your views with evidence from pages 42–49.

If you are on the King's side, point out how the Commons didn't know when to stop but kept on pushing for more and more concessions from the King. They had to be stopped.

If you are on Parliament's side, point out how at each stage it was the King who made things worse. He first brought soldiers to Parliament. He declared war. He must be taught a lesson.

Who fought whom?

IN AUGUST 1642 Charles raised his standard at Nottingham. The Civil War had begun.

In the English Civil War not many people actually chose which side they were going to be on. They supported the side that got its army there first or the side the local lord supported. The ordinary people were then forced to fight for that side. They were also forced to pay taxes to pay for the armies and to provide shelter and food for passing soldiers.

Some history books will give you a map such as Source 1 or a statement such as Source 2 to explain who was fighting on each side.

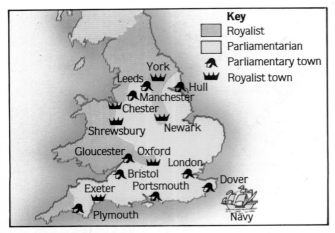

SOURCE 1   From a modern school textbook

SOURCE 2   From a modern school textbook

“If we want to understand the Civil War a glance at the map is important. Support for Parliament came from the rich south and east of England, the King's support from the poor north and west.

Most of the nobles fought for the King and they were joined by the gentry. Religion was also important – Catholics fought for the King and Puritans for Parliament.

Most MPs were against the King. So were the merchants.”

Now compare these interpretations with Sources 3–5.

SOURCE 3   By a modern historian

“The Civil War was fought between two minorities, struggling in a sea of neutralism and apathy.”

SOURCE 4   Recent findings by historians

“■ *Parliament: Nearly half the MPs in the House of Commons fought for the King. The King was supported by MPs from all parts of the country, although Parliament had more supporters from the east and south of England.*

■ *The counties: In each county between a third and two thirds of the gentry seem to have taken no active part in the war. Most of the ordinary people took no part either.*

Many of those listed as supporters of one side or the other were forced to assist one group.

In 21 counties armies were organised to keep both sides out.

In Lancashire 272 of the gentry supported the King, 138 supported Parliament, nine changed sides.

■ *Men and women: The female half of the population contributed nothing to making war break out. Women did fight once the war had started – women of the gentry sometimes had to defend their homes. Women did take the lead to stop the war. At Bristol they threw open the gates to an approaching army to prevent fighting.*”

SOURCE 5   A summary of who supported whom written by Clarendon only twelve years after the event. He was a supporter of the King

“*For Parliament:*
■ *Leeds, Halifax and Bradford: three very rich towns*
■ *the ports*
■ *the common people*
■ *the poorest and lowest of people.*

For the King:
■ *Oxford was the only city in England that Charles could say was entirely on his side*
■ *most of the gentry*
■ *persons of great honour or fortune.*”

1. Do Sources 3 and 4 support Sources 1 and 2?
2. Do you think Source 5 is more reliable than Source 4?
3. Work in groups. Study the evidence on these two pages carefully. Draw up three statements you can all agree on about who supported which side in the Civil War. Make sure you can support your statements using the evidence.

The soldiers

At the start of the war the King's armies were much better equipped than Parliament's. Sources 6 and 7 show the uniforms of ROYALIST soldiers. Parliament's army improved enormously towards the end of the war. Source 8 shows the equipment of a cavalry soldier in Parliament's New Model Army in 1645.

SOURCE 6 A Royalist musketeer

SOURCE 7 A painted glass window from Chester showing members of the King's army in 1646

SOURCE 8 The uniform of a Parliamentary cavalry trooper

1. On your own copy of Sources 6 and 8 label the following features. You will have to decide which of the two sources they apply to:
   - Leather coat (stained with yellow)
   - Iron back and breastplate
   - Calibre belt supporting a gun
   - Shoulder belt supporting a sword
   - Right arm protected by an iron gauntlet
   - Head protected by a 'pot' helmet
   - Stand to support the musket when firing
   - Charges of gunpowder
   - Bullets in a round bag.
2. Would you have felt safer on the battlefield as a Royalist or a Parliamentarian?

What was life like during the Civil War?

CIVIL wars are often very nasty. Communities can be split so that people are fighting against former friends and neighbours. Even families can be split, with children on the opposite side from their own parents, brothers against sisters. Many people are forced into fighting for one side or the other when all they want is peace and to be able to get on with their lives.

People's farms and homes are often destroyed, with many innocent people suffering. Villagers in Worcestershire were told that if they did not pay their taxes, 'Your houses will be pillaged and fired and your persons imprisoned.' Soldiers sent to protect towns often looted the houses and churches for food, horses and valuables.

To find out more about what life was like during the English Civil War we are going to look at the experiences of several different people.

Case study 1:

When did you last see your father?

Source 1 shows a scene from the Civil War. We do not know who the boy and girl are. But it is clear that they have been captured by the enemy. The boy is being questioned. Soon his sister will be questioned too.

SOURCE 1 A nineteenth-century painting entitled *And when did you last see your father?*

Activity

Describe the scene as carefully as you can. Which side is ROYALIST and which PARLIAMENTARIAN? How do you know?

Make up the story behind this picture. You should try and include in it your answers to these questions. Who are the other people shown in the painting? Do the children come from a rich family? Why are the men looking for their father? Is he an important person? How did they get captured? Where is their father? What are the thoughts of the boy and girl at this moment? Are they afraid? What do they think is going to happen to them? What answers do they give?

Case study 2:

Lady Harley defends her castle

Brilliana, Lady Harley, and her husband, Sir Robert Harley, were PURITANS and supporters of Parliament. Sir Robert was an MP and was in London with their son Ned during the years 1642–3. Lady Harley was left to defend her home, Brampton Castle in Herefordshire, as her neighbours turned against her and the ROYALIST forces moved closer.

Her letters to her son Ned show her worries during these two years. She had good reason to worry. When nearby Hopton Castle was taken by Royalists in 1644, the prisoners were tied up and laid on the ground so that their throats could be cut. The bodies were then thrown into a pit.

SOURCE 2 Letters from Lady Harley to her son Ned, July 1642 to January 1643

17 July 1642 I sent Samuel to Hereford to spy on the Royalists. He tells me all at Hereford cried out against your father. I could wish my cousin Adams were out of the house, for I am sure he will give the Royalists what help he can.
19 July I long to see you, but would not have you come down, for I cannot think this country is very safe. I hope your father will give me full directions how I may best have the house guarded. My dear Ned, I thank God I am not afraid. It is the Lord's cause we stand for.
  The boy I have sent to London is such a roguish boy that I dare not keep him in my house. I fear he will join the Royalists.
  I have written to Worcester for 50 weight of shot. I sent to Worcester so I could keep it secret.
13 December I fear our corn and malt will·not hold out if this continues; and they said they will burn my barns; and my fear is that they will place soldiers so near that there will be no going out.
28 January 1643 Mr Wigmore will not let the fowler bring me any fowl, nor will he let any of my servants pass — they dare not go to the town. They have forbidden my rents to be paid. We could be attacked by soldiers any day.

At this stage of the war Lady Harley starts to use a code in some of her letters. The letter in Source 3 has been printed here in a way that shows how the code worked. The words in brackets should be ignored. If you write out the remaining words you will find Lady Harley's message.

SOURCE 3 Letter to Ned, 1 March 1643

I desire you [imagine to] would pray [all strength and] your father [all go together; why did I wrong my judgement so as to] to send me [let us the] word what [world. As for to where I did know] he would have [all be it] me do; if I put [it is strange] away the [there was no hold] men I shall [thirst if] be plundered [once of it] and if I [is] have no [forsaken] rents, I know [I wished that when there] not what [had been] course to [for to have seen] take [in season]. If I leave [but] Brampton [there is no art] all will be [of that] ruined.

Activity

You are Lady Harley. Your code has been broken! Invent a new code and send one of Lady Harley's letters from Source 2 using your new code. See if the person sitting next to you can break your code.

SOURCE 4 An eye-witness account of events at Brampton

26 July There appeared troops of horses facing our castle from a hill on the south side, and 300 foot-soldiers to the east of our castle. Altogether there are 700 enemy. The castle is manned by 50 musketeers.
27 July We fired all day with small shot on each other. They plundered our sheep and cattle.
3 August They began a fire in the town which had soon consumed nearly all the town. This evening they made ten shots against us, which only pierced our battlements but slew none of us so the power of God may be observed.
4 August The parsonage and barns were burnt down.
9 August They planted five great guns against our castle as if they meant to have beaten it to dust.
13 August We found our wall in the west was sore battered. We had to line the walls with earth.
15 August The enemy continued battering with their great gun from the church steeple, our worst friend.
22 August They built breastworks [earth banks] in our gardens; and lay so near to us that their rotten language infected the air.

WHAT WAS LIFE LIKE DURING THE CIVIL WAR?

SOURCE 5 In September it looked as if Lady Harley had been successful

❝*9 September The Lord was this day pleased to take away these bloody villains. Our food had nearly run out, the roof of the castle was so battered that there was not one dry room, yet this noble lady bore all with admirable patience.*❞

But in October the Royalist forces returned and the great guns began to batter the castle once more. Lady Harley held out again, but then died of a bad cold. Early in 1644 the defenders surrendered.

SOURCE 6 The great gun

1. Give three pieces of evidence from Sources 2–5 that show that Lady Harley's neighbours were Royalists.
2. Give three examples of Lady Harley's bravery.
3. Write out a list of all the different methods and weapons used by the Royalists to besiege and attack the castle.
4. What evidence can you find that the people in the castle were sure God was on their side?

Activity

You are a Royalist soldier. In no more than 100 words describe the main events at Brampton between July 1642 and September 1643. Remember that the accounts above were written by people in the castle. You must write your account from the point of view of the Royalists.

Case study 3:
'Plunder and violence'

SOURCE 7 A description of what Prince Rupert's troops did to Birmingham after they had captured it in April 1643 (Rupert was Charles I's nephew)

❝*They ran into every house cursing and damning, threatening and terrifying the poor women most terribly, setting naked swords and pistols to their breasts. They fell to plundering all the town, picking purses and pockets, searching in holes and corners and every other place they could suspect for money or goods. They beastly assaulted many women's chastity, and bragged about it afterwards, how many they had ravished.*

The next day in every street they kindled fire with gunpowder, match, wisps of straw, hay and burning coals.❞

SOURCE 8 A print published during the war showing Royalist soldiers

SOURCE 9 From the title page of a pamphlet called *The Bloody Prince*

54

SOURCE 10 Parliamentary soldiers in a church in 1646

SOURCE 11 A contemporary caricature of a pillaging soldier

1. Look at Source 11. Can you see:
   - the goose instead of a musket
   - a dripping pan instead of a shield
   - bottles of wine hanging from his cross-belt
   - black pots instead of garters
   - an artichoke instead of a sword
   - a tripod pot and a duck on his head instead of a helmet?
2. Compare this soldier with the one in Source 6 on page 51. What are the differences?

SOURCE 12 Part of a letter from Sir Thomas Myddleton to the Speaker of the House of Commons

"*The plundering of the soldiers makes most people hate the very name of a soldier. This has led to a great party in Shropshire, Hereford, Radnor and Montgomeryshire, who call themselves neutrals and have armed themselves to withstand the plunderings.*

I think the common people in all counties will be quickly won over to our side if Parliament declared against plundering and against all Commanders who allow it and do not punish guilty soldiers."

SOURCE 13 The Resolutions of the Clubmen of Dorset, 1645

"*We belong to an Association to preserve ourselves from plunder and violence.*

Until we receive answers from the King and Parliament:
- *The Constable of each town shall set a constant watch of two every night and they shall be well armed.*
- *All soldiers who are caught plundering shall be disarmed and returned to their army.*
- *If lodging is demanded by an army for a soldier he shall be friendly entertained if he behaves himself in his quarters.*
- *Any person assembling soldiers for the King or Parliament will not be given our protection.*"

3. List which of Sources 7–13 were produced by a) Royalists, b) Parliamentarians, c) neutrals. Choose one source from each list and explain why you have put it in that list.
4. Would you say the evidence above supports this statement:
   - 'Many people did not care who won the war as long as they themselves were safe.'

Activity

Divide into pairs. One of you is a Royalist, the other a Parliamentarian. Each of you should design the front page of a pamphlet with words and a drawing showing how terrible the other side's soldiers are. Then compare your pamphlets.

Why did the Royalists lose at Marston Moor?

THERE were very few major battles in the Civil War. However, when a major battle such as Marston Moor did take place it could have a decisive effect on the course of the war.

The background

In 1644 Parliamentary armies were besieging one of the King's strongholds — the city of York. On 14 June Charles sent a letter to his nephew, Prince Rupert, the commander of the main ROYALIST army, asking him to help York.

Prince Rupert marched his army into Yorkshire. You can see his progress in Source 1.

When the Parliamentary commanders, Thomas Fairfax and Oliver Cromwell, heard that Rupert was on his way they moved their armies to Marston Moor, four miles to the west of York. They wanted to bar Rupert's way to York. If Rupert wanted to rescue York he would have to defeat them first.

However, Rupert surprised them by taking his army on a 22-mile forced march on a roundabout route, crossing three rivers, before circling round to make camp just north of York, between the Parliamentarians and the city. He had ended the siege without having to fight a battle.

What should he do now: fight the Parliamentary armies or return south to the King? He decided to fight, even though he was vastly outnumbered. This was because he thought the King had told him to try and defeat the Parliamentary armies as well as saving York.

SOURCE 1 Map showing movements of Rupert's army and the Parliamentary army

The battle

At four o'clock in the morning on 2 July, Prince Rupert surprised the Parliamentarians by marching his army onto Marston Moor. He could have attacked the Parliamentary armies before they were ready, but he waited for the Marquis of Newcastle and his troops to come out of York. They were exhausted from their ten-week siege. They took their time and did not arrive until late afternoon. By then the Parliamentary army was ready and any chance of a surprise attack was gone.

Rupert had a ditch dug and lined it with musketeers. Just behind them he had his cavalry on the flanks and the foot-soldiers in the middle. At seven o'clock in the evening the battle started. Two hours later it was all over.

SOURCE 2 A modern historian has drawn this plan of the start of the battle using written accounts and plans drawn at the time

1. Using Sources 3–7, draw two more plans like Source 2 showing what happened half-way through the battle and the positions at the end. Use arrows to show the movements of each army's different forces. Write a few lines of explanation for each plan.

SOURCE 3 Written by a Parliamentary officer and published three days after the battle

We advanced down the hill through a great field of corn, to a ditch which they controlled. We were losing on the right wing, and gaining on the left.

SOURCE 4 Written by Cromwell's Scoutmaster-General who was on the left with Cromwell

We came down in the bravest order, and with the greatest resolution that ever was seen. In a moment we were past the ditch onto the Moor, upon equal grounds with the enemy.

They soon routed Byron's cavalry, but Rupert came to Byron's rescue.

SOURCE 5 Written by a Parliamentary officer

Cromwell's own division had a hard pull of it, for they were charged by Rupert's bravest men in front and on the flank. They stood at the sword's point a pretty while, hacking one another; but at last (it so pleased God) Cromwell broke through them, scattering them like dust. At the same instant the rest of our horse of that wing had wholly broken Rupert's horse on their right wing.

Back on the Parliamentarians' right wing Fairfax was having trouble, and he was soon driven back by the Royalist cavalry. However, Cromwell's cavalry had now reformed after routing Rupert's forces and was now ready to come to Fairfax's help.

SOURCE 6 By a modern historian

Cromwell led his cavalry between Wilstrop Wood and the rear of the battle and charged Goring's cavalry. Goring now had the enemy in front of him and behind. His cavalry fled.

Cromwell had one last task. Newcastle's foot-soldiers were still resisting in the centre. They fought bravely. Even when Cromwell's men had broken through they fought on. They refused to surrender — all of them except 30 were killed.

The Parliamentary troops then went round the battlefield stripping the bodies of the enemy naked. About 4150 Royalists were dead. Only 300 Parliamentarians died.

SOURCE 7 From a contemporary pamphlet. It shows Rupert hiding in a beanfield after the battle

2. Look at Source 7. Can you see:
   - Rupert's pet dog 'Boy' dead
   - Parliamentary soldiers capturing his baggage and horses and discovering crucifixes?
3. Was this pamphlet published by Royalists or Parliamentarians?
4. Why did the Royalists lose? Was it:
   - Rupert's fault
   - the Marquis of Newcastle's fault
   - the King's fault
   - Cromwell's skill
   - a combination of all these?
   Explain your answer.

Marston Moor was a decisive battle in the Civil War. Cromwell emerged as the most powerful Parliamentary leader. From this position of strength he was able to recruit and train a brand new army, which he called the New Model Army. It was highly disciplined and absolutely determined that Parliament should win the war.

After Marston Moor the Royalists never again looked as if they could win the war, although military action continued around the country for another two years. On 5 May 1646 the King finally surrendered to the Scottish army. The Parliamentarians then held him as a prisoner in Carisbrooke Castle on the Isle of Wight.

Why did the English execute their king?

IN 1648, while Charles was in Carisbrooke Castle negotiating with Parliament, he secretly persuaded the Scots to invade England. The second Civil War broke out. The Royalists were easily defeated, but many people were killed. Parliament no longer trusted Charles. It decided he had to be put on trial for treason. The trial was fixed for 20 January 1649, in Westminster Hall. Many people on Parliament's side were very reluctant to be involved in the trial. Many top lawyers and judges disappeared to their country estates to escape being involved. A High Court of Justice was set up, made up of 135 commissioners, who were really both judges and jury. But on the first day only 68 of the 135 turned up!

SOURCE 1 A picture of the trial

The first day: Saturday 20 January 1649

SOURCE 2 A modern historian's account of Charles at the trial

“*It was a small man who walked into Westminster Hall with short steps and mounted the few steps to the dock. He was dressed entirely in black. His beard was tinged with grey and it was less finely trimmed than it had been. His hair fell down to his shoulders and was still thick, though its lustre had gone and it was streaked with grey. Those who had not seen him since the Civil War would have noticed the sunken eyes and the pouches beneath them. He looked like a man who had suffered. It was the face of one who had fought hard and perhaps knew he had lost. Yet there was a maturity in the face. Nor was it a face of an old or a sick man, and when he spoke people noticed that his stammer had gone.*”

1. What impression does Source 2 give you of Charles — that he was weak and afraid or that he had been through a lot but was brave?

SOURCE 3 A description of the trial by a modern historian

“*At one end of the Hall were the benches for the judges. In the middle, raised above everyone else a little, was John Bradshaw, the President. Down either side of the Hall were lines of soldiers. Opposite the judges was the dock – a wooden enclosure with a crimson chair facing the judges. Behind the dock was a wooden partition separating off the rest of the Hall and guarded by soldiers. The spectators in the rest of the Hall were separated into two groups by soldiers. Around the top were galleries for more important spectators.*”

2. Which of Sources 1 and 4 do you think this historian used to write the description in Source 3? Explain your answer as fully as possible.

OURCE 4 Another picture of the trial

First the charges against Charles were read out
see Source 5).

SOURCE 5

*Charles, trusted with a limited power to govern
according to the laws of the land and to use the
power for the good of the people, has:*
■ *overthrown the rights and liberties of the
people*
■ *taken away the power of Parliament*
■ *levied war against Parliament and the people.*
*Charles Stuart was guilty of all the treasons,
murders, burnings, damages and mischiefs to this
nation committed in the wars.* "

Charles was then asked to say whether he pleaded
innocent or guilty to these charges. He refused to do
his. Instead, he said that the court had no legal right
o try him. Remember that all courts were meant to
·e the king's courts and under his authority.

he second day: Monday 22 January

he second day of the trial started in the same way
s the first day ended, with the court trying to get
harles to plead. An exchange of words then took
·lace between Charles and Bradshaw, the President
·f the court (see Source 6). The spectators erupted
h uproar as Charles was taken away.

SOURCE 6

" **King:** *I do plead for the liberties of England more
than any of you do.*
Bradshaw: *We sit here by the authority of the
Commons of England, which has called your
ancestors to account.*
King: *I deny that! Show me one precedent.*
Bradshaw: *The point is not to be debated by you.*
King: *The Commons of England was never a
court of law.*
Bradshaw: *Confess or deny the charge.*
King: *By what authority do you sit?*
Bradshaw: *Take him away.* "

The third day: Tuesday 23 January

The same happened on the third day. Charles was
taken away after a few minutes.

> **1.** Who do you think was getting the better of
> the argument at this point in the trial,
> Bradshaw or Charles?

Witnesses are heard: 24–27 January

The judges met without Charles. They were worried
because things were not going as they had planned.
Some of the judges were having doubts about the
whole thing! To stiffen their determination it was
decided to hear all the evidence against Charles now.
He would not be allowed to be present. Evidence
against Charles which had been collected from
around the country was read out. There were still
less than half the Commissioners there.

Here are the main points made against Charles:
■ First, Charles was accused of starting the war
against Parliament. Several witnesses described
Charles raising his standard in August 1642 at the
start of the war.
■ A soldier who had changed sides from King to
Parliament during the war claimed that Charles said
to one of his officers, who was mistreating prisoners
after the Royalists had captured Leicester, 'I do not
care if they cut them three times more, for they are
mine enemies.'
■ Evidence was also given about the period when
Charles was a prisoner in Carisbrooke Castle after
the war. A letter from Charles was produced, which
showed that while he was negotiating with
Parliament for a peace settlement he was also asking
his son to raise another army to fight again.

WHY DID THE ENGLISH EXECUTE THEIR KING?

Verdict and sentence: Saturday 27 January

On 27 January the court sat again and Charles was brought before the judges for the verdict and sentence.

Charles was promised that he could make a speech before the verdict was read out. First he said that he wanted to talk to the Houses of Commons and Lords because he had a plan for peace to put to them. This was refused. When he then tried to make a statement Bradshaw would not allow him to. The verdict and the sentence were then read out.

Bradshaw claimed Charles was guilty because it was the duty of the king to see that Parliaments were called frequently. Charles had not done this and so he had attacked the basic liberties of everyone in the country.

> **SOURCE 7** The sentence
>
> *This court does judge that Charles Stuart, a tyrant, traitor, murderer and public enemy of the people, shall be put to death by the severing of his head from his body.*

The execution was fixed for 30 January.

The death warrant still had to be signed. About 40 of the judges signed it without any hesitation, but others had to be forced to sign it. In the end it was signed by only 59 of the original 132 judges!

1. Draw up a list of all the evidence which suggests that Parliament was worried and nervous about putting the King on trial and sentencing him. You might look at the following: whether soldiers were present, whether Charles was allowed to present his case, why there were so many judges.

Activity

Using the evidence on page 58–60, as well as all the evidence you can find about the events of Charles' reign, put Charles on trial. You will need people to take the parts of Charles, Bradshaw and some judges. You will also need witnesses to speak for and against the King. Your teacher will help you prepare your arguments.

Execution: Tuesday 30 January

On the morning of 30 January Charles rose early. He asked for two shirts, since it was cold and he did not want to appear to be shivering from fear. He was then taken to Whitehall, where he ate a piece of bread and drank some wine and then prayed. At two o'clock he stepped onto the scaffold.

> **SOURCE 8** From the diaries of Philip Henry, who was visiting his father in London at the time
>
> *I stood amongst the crowd where the scaffold was erected, and saw what was done, but was not so near as to hear anything. I saw the blow given, I can truly say, with a sad heart. At that instant, I remember well, there was such a groan by the thousands then present, as I never heard before and desire I may never hear again. There was according to order one troop immediately marching from Charing Cross to Westminster and another from Westminster to Charing Cross, purposely to massacre the people, and to disperse and scatter them, so that I had much trouble amongst the rest to escape home without hurt.*

Afterwards, devoted followers of the King and souvenir hunters rushed to dip their handkerchiefs in his blood and to take hairs from his head and beard. The following day the head was sewn back on, and a few days later the body was quietly buried at Windsor Castle.

1. Source 9 shows three separate events taking place on the scaffold. What are they?
2. Describe the different reactions of the people marked A, B, C and D in Sources 9–11.
3. What evidence is there that the painter of Source 10 may have seen Source 9?
4. Why do you think Dutch and French artists were interested in painting this event, as well as English artists?
5. Do you think these sources taken together give us reliable evidence about:
   - where the execution took place
   - who was on the scaffold
   - who was in the crowd
   - whether there were soldiers there
   - how the spectators reacted?

SOURCE 9 A contemporary picture of Charles' execution, by a Dutch artist

SOURCE 10 The execution of Charles, painted by a French contemporary

SOURCE 11 A picture of the execution of Charles made to be printed and sold straight after the event

6. ■ 'The execution of the king was the most important moment in the English Revolution so far.'
   Do you agree with this statement? Give your reasons.

Charles the martyr or Charles the traitor?

Rewriting history

ON THE day of the King's burial a book appeared in London. So many copies were sold that within a year it had to be reprinted 30 times. The book was called *Eikon Basilike* and it was a carefully planned attempt by the Royalists to create a version of Charles and his reign that would show him to be a martyr.

The book was planned while Charles was still alive and Charles had been involved in some of the planning. It was soon widely believed that Charles had written the book himself and it became known as 'the King's book'.

It showed the King as a man who ruled according to God's guidance and who carried out his duties as a Christian king. His enemies had made war on him and were now trying to wash the blood from their own hands by shedding his. He was also shown as a merciful king, who forgave his enemies and who faced his death with great bravery.

SOURCE 1 Charles as shown on cover of the *Eikon Basilike*

1. Look at Source 1. Charles is shown here in royal robes and with a crown of thorns. He is in a beam of light from Heaven. What impression does this give of Charles?

SOURCE 2 An extract from the *Eikon Basilike*, quoting what Charles is supposed to have said

> *[I saw that I might die] a violent, sudden and barbarous death; in the strength of my years; in the midst of my kingdom; my friends and loving subjects being helpless spectators.*

Soon other similar booklets appeared. Many compared the King's execution with Christ's crucifixion. One pamphlet even considered Charles' martyrdom to have been worse than Christ's (see Source 3).

SOURCE 3 From a contemporary pamphlet about Charles' death

> *Even the crucifying of our blessed Saviour did not equal this, and Christ, although as unjustly condemned, was yet judged at a lawful court.*

Pictures of the King like the one in Source 4 were circulating. Stories were told about miracles brought about by scraps of linen stained with his blood.

When Charles II was restored to the throne in 1660 the story of Charles the martyr was completed. The bodies of Oliver Cromwell and other Parliamentarian leaders (known as the regicides – the king killers) were removed from Westminster Abbey and exposed on the gallows at Tyburn. The heads were cut off and put on show.

Those still alive were put on trial and some were executed (see Source 6). During these trials the story of Charles' execution was added to: one Parliamentarian was accused of spitting in his face, another was said to have ordered the King to be tied down at the execution.

During the following years Charles' reputation was radically improved. Even his reign was seen as a wonderful time when everyone was happy.

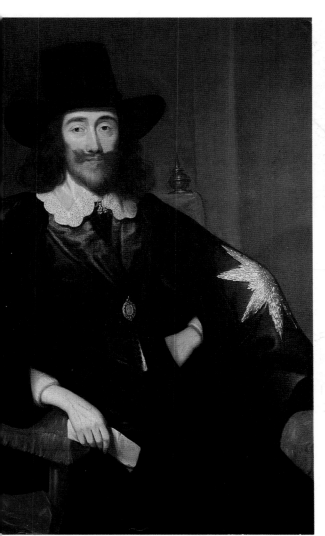

SOURCE 4 Portrait of Charles during his trial by Edward Bower, who made sketches of Charles at the trial and then painted several versions of this picture for various patrons

Activity 1

Work in pairs.

One of you should write an obituary for Charles from the point of view of John Bradshaw in 1649.

The other should write an obituary for Charles from the point of view of a Royalist in 1665.

Each of you should choose one picture from this book to go with your obituary.

Then together write an explanation of why your obituaries are so different.

SOURCE 6 The execution of the regicides, a drawing made in 1660

SOURCE 5 From Clarendon's *History of the Rebellion*

It is most certain, that, in that very hour when he was thus wickedly murdered in the sight of the sun, he had as great a share in the hearts and affections of his subjects in general . . . as any of his predecessors had ever been. To conclude, he was the worthiest gentleman, the best master, the best friend, the best husband, the best father, and the best Christian, that the age in which he lived produced. And even if he were not the best king, . . . no other prince was ever unhappy who was possessed of half his virtues and endowments. "

Activity 2

Being a king or queen in seventeenth-century England was not easy. Design an application form which could be used to find out if possible monarchs had the right qualities.

Then fill it in for Charles I.

What kind of man was Oliver Cromwell?

BETWEEN 1649 and 1660 England had no monarch. For the first time in its history the country was a REPUBLIC. Nobody really knew how to govern the country without a king. There were many experiments to see what kind of government should replace the monarchy.

The most powerful force in the country was the army. So the most powerful person in the country was the one who controlled the army. That was Oliver Cromwell.

Opinions about Cromwell differed a lot at the time and historians still disagree about him today.

■ Some say that during this period Cromwell tried to grab more and more power for himself. Others say he was trying to find a better way of governing.

■ Some say Cromwell believed in giving people greater freedom. Others say he crushed anyone who disagreed with him.

You can decide what you think about Cromwell as we see how Cromwell dealt with a number of problems facing the government between 1649 and 1660.

The Irish rebellion

The Irish Catholics had rebelled against English rule in 1641. According to the English, they had committed many brutal and cruel acts. But nothing could be done about the Irish rebellion until the English Civil War was over.

The Catholics in Ireland supported Charles I's son. They thought he should be King of England and in 1649 the leader of the Irish Catholics, the Marquis of Ormonde, was in France collecting soldiers and weapons. He might launch an invasion from Ireland. As you can see from the map in Source 1 Ireland posed a real threat to Cromwell and his supporters.

In 1649 Cromwell landed in Ireland with an army of 12,000 men. His first target was the town of Drogheda, which was defended by part of Ormonde's army led by Sir Arthur Aston. Sources 2–5 tell you what happened next.

SOURCE 2 Cromwell's letter to the House of Commons, 17 September 1649

❝Our army came to Drogheda on 3 September. On Monday 9th the battering guns began. I sent Sir Arthur Aston a request to surrender the town.

Receiving no satisfactory answer, the guns beat down the corner tower, and opened breaches in the east and south walls.

On Tuesday 10th, after some hot fighting, we entered. Several of the enemy, including Sir Arthur Aston, retreated into Mill Mount, a place very difficult to attack. Our men were ordered by me to put all to the sword. I also forbade them to spare any people in the town who had weapons.

In the great church almost 1000 of them were put to the sword, fleeing there for safety. I think that night we put to the sword in all about 2000 men. This is the righteous judgement of God upon those barbarous wretches who have dipped their hands in so much innocent blood. It will help to prevent bloodshed for the future.

SOURCE 3 An English engraving of the attack

Key

▨ Mainly under Parliament's control

▢ Controlled by Irish rebels

• Drogheda
• Dublin

SOURCE 1 Ireland in 1649

SOURCE 4 Written by Clarendon in 1668–70. He was in France with Charles I's son at the time of the Irish rebellion. He was a friend of Ormonde

The soldiers threw down their arms on an offer of quarter. The enemy entered Mill Mount without resistance. They put every soldier to the sword and all the citizens who were Irish, man, woman and child.

SOURCE 5 From a letter written by the Marquis of Ormonde, 29 September 1649

Cromwell's soldiers promised to spare the lives of any who laid down their arms. But when they had all in their power, the word 'No quarter' went round.

There are two important seventeenth-century rules of warfare you need to know about:
- A successful army could give 'quarter' to the enemy. This meant the enemy surrendered and gave up their weapons. It was then wrong to kill them.
- If an attacking army broke into a town and the defenders did not surrender, they could all be put to death.

1. Which part of Cromwell's account (Source 2) is shown in Source 3?
2. What do Sources 2, 4, and 5 agree about?
3. What do they disagree about?
4. What reasons does Cromwell give for the slaughter?
5. To help you decide which of these three accounts is the most reliable, decide for each source:
   - whether the author was an eye-witness
   - whether other accounts agree with it
   - whether the author had any reason for lying.
6. Now look again at the rules of warfare. If events were as Cromwell described was he justified in what he did?

Cromwell and Parliament

Between 1649 and 1653 England was governed by 'the Rump'. This was what was left of the Long Parliament after all the ROYALISTS had left.

Cromwell hoped that it would pass reforms to make England a more godly place, and to give Protestants freedom to worship as they wished. He then wanted the Rump to organise elections for a new Parliament so voters could choose who they wanted in Parliament. But in fact the Rump did none of these things.

By 1653 Cromwell was very frustrated and decided to get rid of the Rump.

SOURCE 6 An eye-witness account

Lord General Cromwell came to the House. After a while he got up. He spoke of the good things that Parliament had done. Then he began pacing the floor and said, 'You are no Parliament. I say you are no Parliament; I will end your sitting.'

Then he said to Colonel Harrison, 'Call them in,' and twenty or thirty musketeers entered. Then Cromwell, pointing to the Speaker, said to Harrison, 'Fetch him down.'

Cromwell then went to the table where the mace lay and said, 'Take away these baubles.' The soldiers took away the mace. The House went out.

1. Use Source 6 to help you explain what is happening in Source 7. Can you see Cromwell, the soldiers, the Speaker, the MPs?
2. Look back at page 43. How do Cromwell's actions compare to Charles'?

SOURCE 7 The Rump Parliament is dismissed

WHAT KIND OF MAN WAS OLIVER CROMWELL?

The Lord Protector

In 1653 a new Parliament devised a new CONSTITUTION. It decided to give a large share of power to Cromwell. It made him Lord Protector.

SOURCE 8 Written by Bishop Burnet 50 years after the events

Cromwell would rather have taken a shepherd's staff than the Protectorship. Nothing went more against his feelings than a show of greatness. But he saw it was necessary at that time, to keep the nation from falling into extreme disorder.

SOURCE 9 From Clarendon's *History of the Rebellion*

This man, against the desires of all noble persons, took the throne of three kingdoms. Without the name of king, but with a greater power and authority than had been claimed by any king.

1. Look at Source 10.
a) Where is Cromwell?
b) Who appears to be driving the horses?
c) Who has been run over?
d) Why are the three women weeping?
2. Do you think the artist of Source 10 would agree with Clarendon (Source 9) or Burnet (Source 8)?
3. Look at Source 11. Do you agree with Source 9 that Cromwell was more powerful than Charles had been?

▶ **SOURCE 10** Cartoon titled 'Cromwell's chariot'

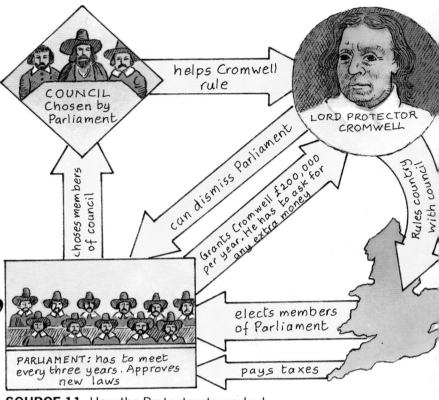

COUNCIL Chosen by Parliament

helps Cromwell rule

LORD PROTECTOR CROMWELL

chooses members of council

can dismiss Parliament

Grants Cromwell £200,000 per year. He has to ask for any extra money

Rules country with council

elects members of Parliament

PARLIAMENT: has to meet every three years. Approves new laws

pays taxes

SOURCE 11 How the Protectorate worked

he 'king'?

1 1654 another new Parliament was elected.
romwell did not get on with it very well. There was
rouble straight away because it wanted to restrict
eople's freedom to worship God as they wished.
romwell insisted that this would not happen. In
655 Cromwell dismissed the Parliament.

He then tried a new experiment. He divided the
ountry into eleven districts. Each one was ruled by a
Major General. They were very unpopular.

By 1657 everyone was running out of ideas about
ow the country could be governed. Many MPs and
entry throughout the country had had enough of
he rule of the army and of the high taxes they had
o pay. They were also worried about the new ideas
hat were threatening their way of life. Some of the
ower classes were claiming that the land belonged
o everybody. Riots had broken out. Where would it
ll end?

Many people thought that the only way to bring
back law and order was to bring back the monarchy.
But they did not want Charles Stuart (Charles I's
on). The one man who could bring about order was
Cromwell. In February 1657 he was offered the
rown.

Cromwell rejected the offer. But he did accept a
new CONSTITUTION. Under this constitution his son
would become Lord Protector after him and some of
the religious freedom given in previous years would
be taken away. There would also be a ceremony, like
a coronation, to 'invest' or recognise the Lord
Protector.

SOURCE 14 Description of Cromwell's investiture
as Lord Protector, June 1657

*As he entered Westminster Hall, His Highness was
dressed in a robe of purple velvet lined with
ermine, being the dress used at the investiture of
princes.*

SOURCE 15 Cromwell, painted in 1650. He told the
artist, 'Paint my picture exactly like me, and do not
flatter me at all, but show all these wrinkles, pimples,
warts and everything as you see me'

SOURCE 12 From the diary of Thomas Burton,
reporting a meeting between Cromwell and army
officers in March 1657. It was written at the time

*One hundred officers said to His Highness
[Cromwell] that he should not take the title of
king because it was not pleasing to his army, it
was a matter of scandal to the people of God, it
was dangerous to his own person, and it would
make way for Charles Stuart to come in again.*

SOURCE 13 From the memoirs of Edmund
Ludlow, written at the time

*Cromwell tried all possible means to persuade the
army officers to approve his plan [to become
king]. He invited himself to dine with General
Fleetwood and Colonel Desborough, where he
began to go on about monarchy. They told him
that those who offered it were friends of Charles
Stuart.*

1. What reasons are given in Sources 12 and 13
against Cromwell accepting the crown?

Activity
Split into two groups. Read through the evidence
about Cromwell on pages 64–67.
■ **Group A** You are enemies of Cromwell. You
want people to believe he wants to make himself
king and take all the power. Use the stories about
Cromwell to design the front page for a
newspaper to convince people of this. Slant your
headlines and stories to prove your point.
■ **Group B** You believe Cromwell is acting in the
best interests of England. He is not interested in
becoming king. Design the front page for a
newspaper to show this. Slant your headlines and
stories to prove your point.

The world turned upside down

AFTER the Civil War new and extreme ideas about how society should be organised began to circulate.

A few years earlier they would not have been allowed. But people were now freer to say what they liked. Anyone with a printing press could publish pamphlets. These new ideas were supported by only a small number of people at the time, but many people — gentry, MPs and ordinary people, too — felt very threatened by them. Some of the ideas went too far even for Cromwell, as you will see.

The Diggers

Scattered across south and east England were small groups of people known as 'Diggers'.

Their leader, Gerald Winstanley, said that God made the earth for everyone to share. They believed that 'No one branch of mankind should rule over another. The poorest man has as much right to the land as the richest man.'

Winstanley and a group of Diggers moved onto common land at St George's Hill in Surrey. They claimed that it belonged to the people, not to the lords. If these areas were farmed it would solve England's food problems and get rid of poverty.

Cromwell and the army were tolerant towards them, but the local landowners and MPs were not pleased. Concern increased when Diggers started to travel around the country to win support.

Parliament produced PROPAGANDA against them and in 1650 the local landowners and clergy drove the Diggers away from St George's Hill.

Women try to be heard

In 1649 a group of women petitioned Parliament.

> **SOURCE 1** The women's petition
>
> 66 We desire a share in the freedoms of this state. Have we not an equal interest with the men of this nation? Are our lives, rights or goods to be taken from us more than from men? And can you imagine us to be so stupid as not to see when [our rights] are being daily broken down? 99

> **SOURCE 2** Parliament's reply
>
> 66 The House gave an answer to your husbands. Go home and meddle with your housewifery.
> It is fitter for you to be washing your dishes. Things are brought to a fine pass if women teach Parliament how to make laws. 99

SOURCE 3 'Skimmington beats her husband'. This print from 1639 shows what people feared would happen if society changed too much

1. Did Parliament see women as a danger or as a silly nuisance?
2. If somebody used Parliament's arguments in Source 2 today, how would you reply to them?
3. What do Sources 1–3 tell you about the position of women in the seventeenth century?

The Fifth Monarchists

Many people in the seventeenth century believed that the forces of Christ were in a constant battle with the Devil (who was represented by the Roman Catholic Church).

The Fifth Monarchists believed Christ was about to win the battle. When he did he would come and rule the earth as the 'Fifth Great Monarch'. Their job, therefore, was to make England a godly place for Christ to come to.

Many of their members were London cloth workers and craftsmen. They particularly disliked the gentry and refused to take off their hats when meeting those who were higher up the social scale. Being 'godly' was more important than being a gentleman.

They did not believe in being ruled by elected MPs. They thought a Parliament of godly people should rule. They wanted reforms of the legal system, such as getting thieves to work for the people they stole from rather than being hanged.

The Levellers

The Levellers probably had more support than any of the other groups. After the bad harvest and high prices of the winter of 1649 the Levellers won a lot of support from soldiers, who were owed a lot of money by Parliament, and from poor people, who were hardest hit by bad harvests and high prices.

> **SOURCE 4** Some of the Levellers' demands, May 1649
>
> ■ *That the Supreme Authority of England shall be a Parliament of 400 persons. It should be chosen by all men of 21 years of age and over (except those who are servants, or receive poor relief or who fought for the King)*
> ■ *no accused person may be forced to give evidence against themselves*
> ■ *no imprisonment for debt*
> ■ *execution only for murder*
> ■ *parishioners should be able to choose their own ministers*
> ■ *no customs duties. All money should be raised by taxing property*
> ■ *trial by jury*
> ■ *no tithes*
> ■ *freedom of worship.*

John Lilburne was leader of the Levellers. In Charles I's reign he had been whipped through the streets when he criticised Archbishop Laud.

In 1649, when he criticised Cromwell and the Rump Parliament, he was arrested and tried for treason. The jury found him innocent.

In 1651 the Rump banished him from the country, but he returned in 1653 and was put in prison until he died in 1657.

The Levellers did not have Cromwell's support. He wanted to keep strict discipline in the army, but in May 1649 the Levellers in the army led a mutiny. Over 1000 of them gathered at the village of Burford. Cromwell did not hesitate. He attacked and

they were easily defeated. But although all of the Levellers were sentenced to death, in the end only four of the leaders were executed.

After this the movement lost support and slowly faded away. Many of the soldiers received the pay they were owed and economic conditions for ordinary people improved.

---

1. Make two lists showing the ideas put forward by the four groups. One list should contain the ideas that would be accepted today, and the other list the ideas that would not be.
2. In a class discussion, try to decide which of the groups would have been definitely for and which definitely against
   ■ democracy
   ■ the Catholic Church
   ■ reforming the legal system
   ■ sharing all the land between everyone.

SOURCE 5 The world turned upside down – a cartoon drawn in 1647 by 'a well-wisher to the King'

---

3. Look at Source 5. What is upside down?
4. What do you think the artist means by the picture?

Activity

It is 1650. You are a member of the gentry. Which of these groups are you most worried about, and which are you least worried about?

Write a letter to your MP explaining your views.

James II – the same old story?

ON 3 SEPTEMBER 1658 Cromwell died. His son Richard was not strong enough to hold the rival parties in Parliament together. He did not really want to be Lord Protector. So in May 1659 he was forced out of the job by the army and returned to being a farmer. In 1660 the army, with the agreement of most MPs and ordinary people, invited Charles Stuart to return as king. He accepted, and England had a monarchy again.

Charles II was given all the powers his father had had in September 1641. All the laws passed between 1641 and 1660 were declared illegal. The Church of England was brought back. Bishops were appointed. Many of Cromwell's supporters were punished.

In 1685 Charles II died. On his death-bed he declared himself a Catholic. He was succeeded by his brother James, who everybody knew was a Catholic. Three years later James II was driven from the country in what was called the 'Glorious Revolution'.

Opinions about James are divided. Some people think he was like Charles I, or even Mary Tudor. He wanted the Catholics to take over England. Given the chance he would have persecuted Protestants and got rid of Parliament.

Others think he did in fact believe in religious toleration, but failed to make this clear and made some silly mistakes.

> 1. Look at Source 1. Do these actions make you think James wanted England to be Catholic? Or did he just want to give everyone religious freedom?

In June 1688 James' Queen claimed to give birth to a son. James was in his 50s and she had already had several miscarriages, so it was thought she would not be able to have a child. Stories spread that the baby had actually been smuggled into the palace in a warming pan (a pan usually filled with coals to warm the bed).

> 2. People were ready to believe these stories at the time. Why do you think this was?

James now had a son and could make sure he would be followed by a Catholic king. There was a real chance Catholicism could be brought back. Some people began to look around for an alternative king.

In June 1688 powerful Protestants in England asked James' daughter and son-in-law, William and Mary of Orange, to come to England as king and queen.

In November William landed at Torbay and began to move on London. James' army began to desert.

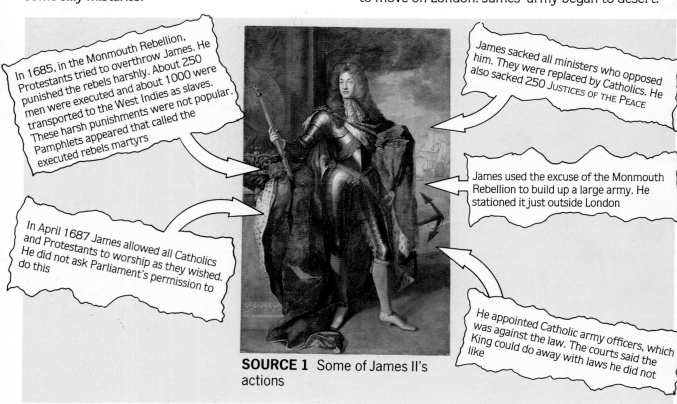

In 1685, in the Monmouth Rebellion, Protestants tried to overthrow James. He punished the rebels harshly. About 250 men were executed and about 1000 were transported to the West Indies as slaves. These harsh punishments were not popular. Pamphlets appeared that called the executed rebels martyrs

James sacked all ministers who opposed him. They were replaced by Catholics. He also sacked 250 JUSTICES OF THE PEACE

James used the excuse of the Monmouth Rebellion to build up a large army. He stationed it just outside London

In April 1687 James allowed all Catholics and Protestants to worship as they wished. He did not ask Parliament's permission to do this

He appointed Catholic army officers, which was against the law. The courts said the King could do away with laws he did not like

SOURCE 1 Some of James II's actions

On 11 December James lost his nerve and left London. He boarded a boat for France, which ran aground off the Kent coast. Some fishermen arrested him, mistaking him for a priest fleeing the country. He was then returned to London.

Meanwhile, William was moving near to London. He ordered that James should be allowed to escape. On 19 December James fled to France. This was exactly what William had hoped he would do.

3. Why didn't William want James captured?
4. Look at Source 2. Which figures are James, William and Mary? Explain how you know.

SOURCE 2 Dutch engraving of the Revolution of 1688

King and Parliament

One of the cartoons in Source 3 shows the relationship between king and Parliament in 1500, in the time of Henry VII. The other shows it in 1700, in the reign of William and Mary. You will easily spot which is which.

SOURCE 3 The changed relationship between king and Parliament, 1500–1700

'Chosen' by God
Can rule without Parliament
Is a Catholic
Rules with ministers' help
Controls the army

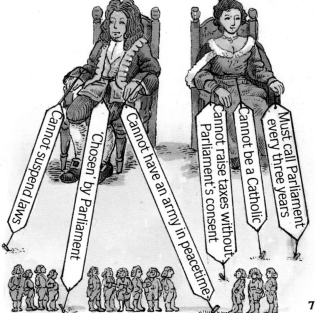

Cannot suspend laws
'Chosen' by Parliament
Cannot have an army in peacetime
Cannot raise taxes without Parliament's consent
Cannot be a Catholic
Must call Parliament every three years

71

Uniting the kingdom

IN 1500 the British Isles consisted of one reasonably strong kingdom, England, two weak ones, Ireland and Scotland, and Wales, which was partly controlled by England and partly run by independent princes. Britain was disunited. As separate nations England, Ireland, Scotland and Wales were weak in comparison with great powers such as France and Spain.

By 1750, however, these four nations were largely under the control of the government in London, and were called the United Kingdom. This unity helped Britain to develop an empire which made it the most powerful force in the world. How had this come about?

---

1. Study the information on this page. On a map of the British Isles that your teacher will give you, write labels to show the factors that were making England, Ireland, Scotland and Wales disunited in 1500.
2. Study the timeline in Source 2. Select five important steps towards the union of Scotland and England.
3. Select five important stages in the English gaining control over Ireland.
4. Was Ireland or Scotland more under English control by 1750? Give reasons for your answer.
5. Look at the maps in Sources 3–5. They show the British Isles in 1543, 1603 and 1707. Explain which is which.

The disunited kingdom

England and Scotland

England and Scotland had been enemies for a long time. The border area between the two countries had been a hotbed of lawlessness for centuries.

This position became more serious in the 1500s, when the Scots and the French joined together to fight against the English. The rulers of France and Scotland were both Catholic, while England was becoming Protestant.

One Scottish monarch, Mary Queen of Scots, was even married to the French king. What's more, she also claimed the English throne. In 1587 there was a rebellion in England by her Catholic supporters. They tried to make Mary Queen of England in place of Elizabeth.

England and Wales

In 1500 the word 'Wales' was not even an accepted geographical expression. What we now know as Wales was divided into the Principality of Wales and the Marcher lordships (see Source 1).

Edward I had set up the Principality of Wales in 1284. It was supposed to be under the king's control, but even in 1500 there was still much lawlessness in these areas.

The Marcher lords ran their own lands (lordships) as independent princes. They recognised no superior authority.

Henry VII revived the old council in Wales in an attempt to rule the country, but in no way could it be said that Wales was under the control of the English monarchy.

England and Ireland

The Protestant Reformation that changed England so much did not take hold in Ireland. Throughout the sixteenth and seventeenth centuries deep divisions remained between the Irish people, who were Catholics, and their English rulers, who were Protestants.

Ireland was a real danger to England because Catholic countries such as France were ready to help the Irish rebels against the English. From 1590 to 1691 there were a number of attempts by English rulers to conquer Ireland for good.

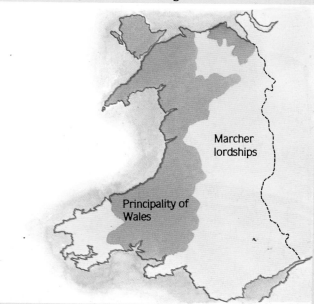

SOURCE 1 Wales in 1500

1534 Henry VIII breaks with the Catholic Church. The Irish remain Catholic

1535 An Irish revolt is put down by the English

1537 An Act of Parliament is passed forcing everyone in Ireland to speak English

1549 A special edition of the Protestant Prayer Book is prepared for the Welsh and the Irish in their own language

1558 Mary Queen of Scots marries Francis, soon to be King of France

1587 Catholics plot to make Mary Queen of England in place of Elizabeth. The rebellion fails. It leads to Mary's execution

1601 Catholic rebels, supported by Spain, are defeated in Ireland. Elizabeth takes land from Catholics and gives it to her Protestant supporters

1638 Riots break out in Scotland against the introduction of the English Prayer Book. The Scots invade northern England

1649 Oliver Cromwell orders massacres of Catholics in Ireland

1689 English army invades Ireland

1707 An Act of Union between England and Scotland is passed. The two countries now share the same Parliament and government. This union is not accepted by the Highlanders in Scotland

SOURCE 2 Some key events in the unification of the United Kingdom

1500

1536 and 1543 Acts of Union between Wales and England are passed by the English government. They simply make Wales part of England. English law now applies throughout the country. Wales also elects MPs to Parliament in London just as all regions of England do. No attempt is made to force the Welsh to use the English language. Welsh language and culture flourish, so Wales is still different from England

1560 Francis dies. Mary returns to Scotland. Protestants depose her from the Scottish throne

1595 Catholic rebellion begins in Ireland

1600

1603 Mary Queen of Scots' son James, King of Scotland, becomes King of England as well. But England and Scotland keep their own Parliaments and are still separate countries

1641 Irish Catholics rebel with much burning, looting and murder

1650 Irish Catholics lose their land. It is given to English Protestants

1691 English army finally defeats the Irish army and the French army that has been supporting the Irish rebels. Protestants now rule Ireland in their own Parliament

1700

1715 A Scottish rebellion is defeated

1745 Another Scottish rebellion is defeated

Key

Under the control of the king, sends MPs to Parliament

Under the control of the king, does not send MPs to Parliament

Not under the control of the king, and does not send MPs to Parliament

SOURCE 3

SOURCE 4

SOURCE 5

73

How united was the United Kingdom?

The Jacobite rebellion

BY THE eighteenth century England, Wales and Scotland were together called the United Kingdom. But was it a suitable name? Was the United Kingdom really united?

In 1745 Charles Edward Stuart ('Bonnie Prince Charlie') led some Scots in a failed attempt to put his father, James, and the STUART family back on the throne. We are going to investigate whether this JACOBITE rebellion showed Scottish unhappiness with the union with England.

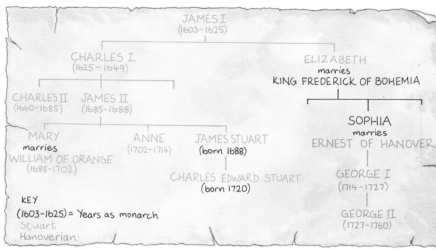

SOURCE 1 Family tree showing the Stuarts' and the Hanoverians' claims to the throne

> 1. Look at Source 1. Who do you think had the better claim to the throne: James Stuart or King George II?

The background

Sources 2 and 3 show the state that Scotland was in prior to the 1745 rebellion.

SOURCE 2 By an eighteenth-century Scottish writer

"For some time before the Rebellion the nation had been in ferment. The many and heavy taxes, and the attacks on our trade by the Spanish, led the government to be attacked by all the newspapers. Our enemies abroad and the unthinking multitude at home were made to believe that the whole nation was ripe for a revolt."

SOURCE 3 By a modern Scottish historian

"In 1690 Scotland had an underdeveloped economy. After the Union with England in 1707 the economy began to develop. The production of linen cloth for export to England grew rapidly. Scotland imported tobacco from America and re-sold it at a profit to France. Technological advances in England quickly spread to be used by Scots industrialists. In 1695 the Royal Bank of Scotland was set up. New farming techniques were being used, more land was farmed and more and more cattle were sold to England.

In July 1745 Bonnie Prince Charlie landed on the small island of Eriskay, off the west coast of Scotland. He had just seven men with him. Did he have a chance of success?

Bonnie Prince Charlie believed that people in the Lowlands of Scotland disliked English rule. However, his best chance of support came from the Highlanders, who were Catholic.

The Highlanders all belonged to clans, or tribes. All the men of a clan could be called to fight by their chief. Source 4 shows you the fighting strength of the biggest of the Highland clans. Charlie believed that the clans were just waiting for an excuse to fight the English. Almost all the English troops were away fighting in France. There were only a few English regiments in Scotland and they had never fought a war. They would be no match for the Highland clans if it came to battle.

SOURCE 4 Fighting strength of the biggest Highland clans

Campbells	5000
MacKenzies	2000
Grants	850
Camerons	800
Mackintoshes	800
Frasers	900
Mackays	800
19 other clans	6800 total
Total	**17950**

If Bonnie Prince Charlie could gain a quick advantage over the English troops he believed many people in Scotland and others in France would quickly come to his support.

1. Why did Charlie think he might be successful?
2. Can you see any reasons in Sources 2 and 3 why he might *not* get the support he expected from Scotland?

▶ **SOURCE 5** Bonnie Prince Charlie landing in Scotland – an engraving made in 1850

Gathering support

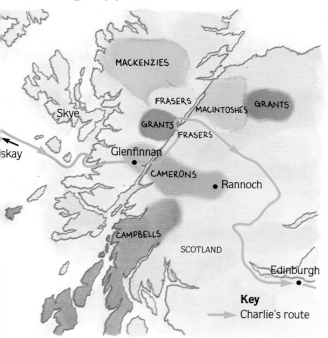

SOURCE 6 Map showing details of Charlie's movements

In August 1745 Bonnie Prince Charlie raised his standard at Glenfinnan, on the west coast of Scotland. By now he had over 200 men with him.

Charlie set about winning support in the Highlands and was joined by some of the large clans: the Camerons, the Mackintoshes and the Frasers. Other smaller clans joined him too, so he had about 4000 fighting men.

SOURCE 7 Why some of the Camerons supported Charlie, as reported by an eye-witness

❝On 15 August five heads of the Camerons entered Rannoch. Their supporters went from house to house and told all the Camerons that if they did not join with them they would that instant proceed to burn all their houses and cattle.❞

1. Refer back to Source 4. How many soldiers did Charlie get from the bigger clans?
2. Would you say that most of the Highlanders supported him?

Edinburgh

The Jacobites marched to Edinburgh and captured it without much trouble. They expected to double the size of their army in Edinburgh. The Prince sent one of his officers, Lord Elcho, to the magistrates of Edinburgh to demand 1000 tents, 2000 targets, 6000 pairs of shoes and 6000 water canteens. He received 2000 targets and 500 tents.

SOURCE 8 A description of the army as it left Edinburgh

❝They exceeded 5500. Of the whole number, not quite 4000 were real Highlanders, who were indeed the strength of the rebel army.❞

1. Did Charlie get much support from Edinburgh?

Into England

The JACOBITE army then left Edinburgh. They won a great victory at Prestonpans. Charlie now seemed to have Scotland at his mercy.

Then, against the advice of his generals, he marched into England. He was sure he had a lot of support there. Sources 9 and 10 tell us what happened as the army crossed into England.

> **SOURCE 9** Written by Lord Elcho
>
> *The army at leaving Edinburgh was 5500 and at Carlisle only 4500.*

> **SOURCE 10** From the *Evening Courant* newspaper, 8 November 1745
>
> *Deserters swarm daily from the Highland army.*

SOURCE 11 The movements of the rebels

As you can see from Source 11, the army marched deeper and deeper into England and by 4 December had reached Derby, only 130 miles from London! But almost no one in England had joined them. The weather was getting colder. Food was short. Many of the men did not like being this far from Scotland. Government armies were closing in, outnumbering them by six to one.

> **SOURCE 12** An eye-witness description of the army as it arrived in Derby
>
> *They were in general a crew of shabby, lousy, pitiful fellows, mixed up with old men and boys, and some without shoes. They appeared more like chimney-sweepers than soldiers.*

The retreat

At Derby Charlie held a meeting with his generals to decide what to do. What would you do in his situation?

> **SOURCE 13** An account of the meeting by Lord George Murray, one of Charlie's officers
>
> *Every officer except the Duke of Perth declared for a retreat. As all the officers agreed in this opinion His Royal Highness said he would consent to it, though he was much disappointed to be so near London and yet not in a condition to march forwards.*

The army had a terrible march back to Scotland. They were followed all the way by the Duke of Cumberland and the main government army. But before Cumberland caught up with him Charlie met up with a second government army, recruited in Scotland. The Jacobites beat this army at the Battle of Falkirk, but after the battle his generals sent him the letter in Source 14.

> **SOURCE 14** Letter to Charlie from his generals, 29 January 1746
>
> *We are certain that a vast number of soldiers are gone home since the Battle of Falkirk. If the enemy should march against us we can foresee nothing but utter destruction. There is no way out of danger but to retire to the Highlands. In spring an army of 10,000 can be brought together.*

The army retreated to the Highlands. Many men went home and did not return. In April 1746 Cumberland's army caught the Jacobites at Culloden. The government army outnumbered the Jacobites by 9000 to 5000. It was better armed and trained and had powerful cannon. The Jacobites were totally defeated.

SOURCE 15 Lord George Murray explains why they lost in a letter to Charlie on 19 April

It was highly wrong to set up the royal standard without knowing that the King of France would assist you.

It was a fatal error to allow the enemy such good positions for their cavalry and cannon.

The last three days before the battle our army was starved.

1. Here are some possible explanations for why the rebellion failed. Choose one or more which you think are correct and give your reasons for your choice.
   ■ The whole enterprise never stood a chance from the beginning.
   ■ Not enough people in Scotland supported Charlie.
   ■ The decision to march into England was a disastrous mistake.
   ■ Mistakes were made at the Battle of Culloden. Until then Bonnie Prince Charlie stood a good chance of winning.

▼ **SOURCE 16** A 'Wanted' poster for Charlie. The reward for catching him is £30,000, a huge sum of money in those days

After the rebellion

After the Battle of Culloden Cumberland's army rampaged through the Highlands killing and plundering.

Charlie was now a wanted man and had to flee. For five months he was hunted down in the Highlands and Islands of Scotland. Poor crofters sheltered him. Flora MacDonald helped him escape from government soldiers by dressing him up as a servant woman. He was rowed twenty miles from the Hebrides to the Isle of Skye and from there taken to France.

SOURCE 17 The *Skye Boat Song*, a traditional ballad

"Speed bonnie boat, like a bird on the wing,
Onward, the sailors cry;
Carry the lad that's born to be king
Over the sea to Skye.
Burned are our homes, exile and death
Scatter the loyal men;
Yet ere the sword cool in the sheath
Charlie will come again."

1. Bonnie Prince Charlie has become a romantic hero. Can you see reasons why this has happened?
2. What other interpretations of Charlie's character would be possible from the evidence on these pages?

Activity
Work in groups. You are organising a 'This is your life' programme for Bonnie Prince Charlie. Write the script, including details of who you will invite to speak and what they will say about Charlie. Then act it out for the rest of the class.

Science and superstition

SOURCE 1 An experiment with an air pump, painted by Joseph Wright of Derby in the 1760s

SOURCE 1 was painted in the middle of the eighteenth century. A scientific experiment like this would have been unthinkable in 1500. In 1750 it was commonplace.

The Scientific Revolution

The changes that took place in the seventeenth century have been called a 'Scientific Revolution'. Is this a good description? To answer this question we need to know what the situation was in 1500.

In 1500 most people thought that the earth was at the centre of the universe. The sun and the planets were fixed to enormous crystal spheres that orbited the earth.

They also believed God controlled the movement of these spheres. Indeed, He controlled everything — for example whether there was a bad harvest or a good one, or whether or not your child survived childbirth. So the best way of finding out about the world was by reading the Bible, or studying the spheres.

People did not really know very much even about their own bodies. Doctors relied on books written by Greek and Roman writers centuries earlier to tell them how the body worked. These books had some good advice in them, but also some bad mistakes. But in 1500 most people didn't realise the books were wrong.

There wasn't even much chance for doctors to find out if the books were right. They were not allowed to dissect corpses and look at their insides, because religion taught that dead people needed their bodies intact for their life in Heaven or Hell. So to cut up a body was a great sin.

In 1500 doctors believed that bodies were made up of four 'humours' — blood, phlegm, yellow bile and black bile. They thought that illnesses were caused when the four humours in a patient got out of balance or one of the humours got poisoned. So to cure their patients they might, for example, drain away some of their blood.

The most common killer diseases were plague, smallpox, typhoid and measles, yet nobody knew what caused them. They didn't know about germs or bacteria.

As the timeline opposite shows, many of these things began to change between 1500 and 1750.

Activity

Write a description of what is happening in Source 1. Who is doing the experiment? Who are all the people watching? What do you think is happening in the glass jar? What are the young children feeling? What is the old man feeling? What is the man by the window doing? Do you think the scientist will let the bird die?

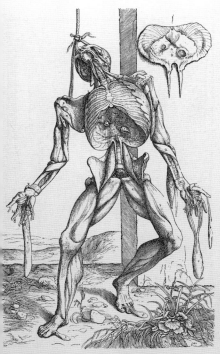

SOURCE 2 One of Vesalius' drawings. He insisted that every doctor should do dissections himself to learn about the human body

1543 In Italy Vesalius, a doctor, publishes accurate drawings of the human body.

1575 A French army surgeon, Paré, recommends that wounds be treated with bandages to prevent infection

1610 In Italy Galileo shows the earth is not at the centre of the universe. He proves that the earth goes round the sun

1613 New river scheme carries clean water 38 miles to the rapidly expanding city of London

1628 In London William Harvey proves that blood circulates continuously around the body. Doctors begin to experiment with blood transfusions

1630 East Anglian Fens are drained, with Dutch help, to make good farming land

1661 In London Boyle uses air pumps to discover that air is essential for breathing and for burning (see Source 1).

1662 Royal Society is founded to help scientists to share their discoveries with one another.

1680s New mechanical looms introduced that weave cloth four times as fast as hand looms.

1686 In London Isaac Newton publishes his *Principia*, the most important scientific book yet published. It shows that there are natural laws which keep the universe going.

1698 First steam engine developed by Thomas Savery to pump water from tin mines in Cornwall

1717 Lady Mary Wortley introduces smallpox inoculation to Britain. A test is made on six orphans, and when they survive the king's grandchildren are successfully inoculated.

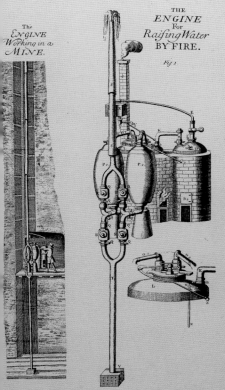

SOURCE 3 Savery's mine pump

SOURCE 4 Galileo developed a powerful telescope. Astronomers could now see the stars and planets much more clearly

1. Tie ligature round upper arm and block vein with right finger

2. With left finger, push blood in the direction of the arrow

3. Remove left finger

4. Can you push the blood back in the direction of the arrow?

SOURCE 5 Harvey's experiment

1. Choose a development that would:
   - improve farming or food supply
   - make people more healthy
   - help scientists understand the world
   - help industry.
2. Look back at the description of science in 1500. What had changed by 1750? What had not changed?

SCIENCE AND SUPERSTITION

Case study 1:

Medicine and health

Did these changes affect the lives of ordinary people? Look at Sources 6–8. They show various ways that ill people could get help in the seventeenth century.

■ People believed that the king or queen, as God's chosen ruler, could cure disease. In Source 6 they want King Charles to cure them of scrofula, a common disease which gave you swollen glands. The last time the royal touch was given was in 1714.

■ Doctors (Source 8) and apothecaries (Source 7) provided a service that changed very little over the period 1500–1750. The apothecary was a shopkeeper who sold all sorts of groceries, as well as perfumes and spices. He mixed his own medicines, which included spices and secret ingredients.

■ In the eighteenth century the newspapers were full of adverts for new remedies such as Dr James' Powders. Many of them were entirely useless. Dr James made a fortune out of his powders, selling 1,612,800 doses over twenty years.

1. Look at Source 8. It shows various things that a doctor would do. Find:
   ■ an amputation
   ■ letting blood
   ■ inspecting urine
   ■ checking for a breast tumour
   ■ extracting a tooth
   ■ repairing a dislocated shoulder.
2. What do you think the remaining scene shows?
3. Why might the activities shown be more dangerous or more painful than they would be today?

SOURCE 6 King Charles II gives the royal touch in 1684

SOURCE 7 An apothecary at work

ALTISSIMVS CREAVIT DE TERRA MEDECINAMET VIR

SOURCE 8 A signboard made in 1623 to hang outside a doctor's surger

Case study 2:
The witch hunts

Look at Source 9. It is 1612, and Mary Sutton has been accused of being a witch. Her hands have been tied together in the shape of a cross. She is being lowered into the water. The people accusing her say that if she sinks she is innocent, if she floats she is guilty.

In the Middle Ages people thought a lot about Heaven and Hell, but they were not really worried about witches. Then, in the sixteenth and seventeenth centuries, people started finding witches everywhere. Just as God had priests to do his work, so people believed the Devil also had 'servants' – called witches. The Devil used his witches to bring all sorts of trouble to good Christians. Witches could make their victims fall ill or die, and they could harm their crops or cattle.

King James I was very interested in witchcraft. In 1590 he had written a book on it and had suggested ways to identify a witch. One of them is shown in Source 9. He said that another way to recognise a witch was by a mark on the witch's body, because at night the Devil would come and visit the witch in the form of a pet and suck the witch's blood.

Laws were passed that allowed witches to be tried in the courts. In 1604 witchcraft became a crime punishable by death. There were more cases of witchcraft in the Essex courts than of any other crime, apart from theft. Hundreds of witches were hanged all around England – the last one as late as 1727. And for every case that came to court there were many more accusations of witchcraft in the villages that never got to court. Most of the people accused were old women.

SOURCE 9 Contemporary engraving of the 'trial' of Mary Sutton

Anyone could accuse anyone else of 'bewitching' them. Anything that went wrong in your life – from a sick cow to the death of a child – could be blamed on witchcraft. The most ridiculous accusations were believed.

SOURCE 10 Extracts from the trial and confession of Joan Williford in 1645

About seven years ago the Devil did appear to Joan Williford in the shape of a little dog. He asked her to give up God and turn to him instead. The Devil promised her money.

She called the Devil 'Bunnie'. She said Bunnie pushed Thomas Gardler out of the window and into the cesspool.

She gave some of her blood to the Devil, who promised to serve her for twenty years. Since she has been in prison she has seen the Devil twice. He has tried to suck her. The devil came to her disguised as a mouse.

SOURCE 11 An examination of a witch in Newcastle in 1649

He laid her body naked to the waist, with her clothes over her head. With fright and shame all her blood ran to one part of her body. He ran a pin into her thigh, and suddenly let her clothes fall and asked her why she did not bleed. Then he took out the pin and set her aside as a child of the Devil.

1. Look at Sources 9 and 11. They both show methods of trying witches. Were these methods fair?
2. Look at Source 10. Why do you think people were ready to believe stories such as these?

Activity
Witch-hunters were paid £1 for every witch they discovered. Design an advert for the job of witch-hunter.

1. Historians only usually talk about a revolution if things change rapidly and have consequences for everyone. Do you think there was a 'Scientific Revolution' in the seventeenth century?

How did London change?

London in the 1500s

THE reconstruction in Source 1 gives you some idea of what London was like in 1500. The buildings were made of wood and plaster and were built so close to each other that it was possible to walk around large parts of London on the rooftops. There had been no street planning when the houses were built and the city as a whole was a chaotic maze of streets and buildings.

There were some grand palaces owned by the very rich and a few big houses built by prosperous merchants (see Source 3).

► **SOURCE 1** London in the 1500s

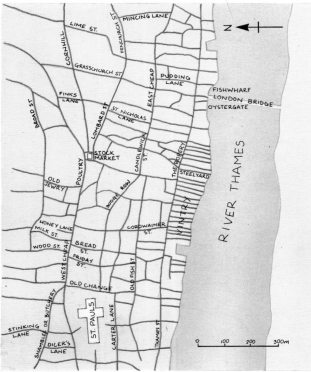

SOURCE 2 The commercial districts of London

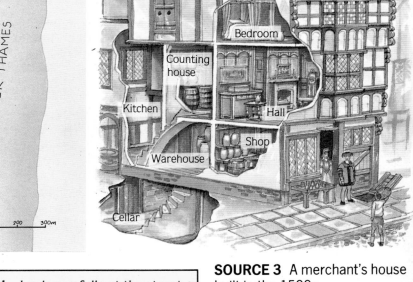

SOURCE 3 A merchant's house built in the 1500s

1. Look carefully at the street names in Source 2. Use them to make a list of all the occupations that were carried out in this area of London.

2. Write a detailed description of the merchant's house in Source 3.

1. Look at Source 4. How many people died in this week?
2. Which were the three most common causes of death?
3. Which causes of death do not kill today?
4. Can you explain what is meant by: 'found dead', 'aged' and 'teeth' as causes of death?

The Plague

Between 1500 and 1700 the population of London grew from 120,000 to 500,000. In 1500 four per cent of the English population lived there, in 1700 it was ten per cent. This growth is remarkable because London was frequently hit by Plague. Nearly 40,000 people (a quarter of the population) died in 1563, and 25,000 in both 1603 and 1625.

Londoners were used to regular visits by the Plague, but in 1665 one of the worst epidemics ever broke out and 80,000 people died.

Source 5 describes one person's view of what life in London during the Plague of 1665 was like.

> **SOURCE 5** Extracts from Samuel Pepys' diary, 1665
>
> **7 June** This day I did in Drury Lane see two or three houses marked with a red cross upon the doors and 'Lord Have Mercy Upon Us' writ there. This worried me so much that I bought a roll of tobacco to smell and chew.
>
> **29 June** Travelled by water to Whitehall, where the Court was full of waggons and people ready to go out of town.
>
> **20 July** Walked home past Radcliffe, where I hear the sickness is scattered almost everywhere. There were 1089 dying of the Plague this week. My Lady Carteret did give me a bottle of plague water.
>
> **12 August** My Lord Mayor commands people to be inside by nine at night that the sick may leave their homes for air and exercise.
>
> **31 August** 6102 died of the Plague this week. But it is feared that the true number is near 10,000, partly from the poor that cannot be taken notice of.
>
> **3 September** Dared not wear my new periwig, bought in Westminster where the Plague is. Nobody will dare buy any hair for fear of infection, that it had been cut off the heads of people dead from the Plague.
>
> **20 September** But, Lord! What a sad time it is to see no boats on the river, and the grass grows all up and down Whitehall court and nobody but poor wretches in the streets.

The Diseases and Casualties this Week.

Cause	No.	Cause	No.
Abortive	6	Kingſevil	10
Aged	54	Lethargy	1
Apoplexie	1	Murthered at Stepney	1
Bedridden	1	Palſie	2
Cancer	2	Plague	3880
Childbed	23	Pluriſie	1
Chriſomes	15	Quinſie	6
Collick	1	Rickets	23
Conſumption	174	Riſing of the Lights	19
Convulſion	88	Rupture	2
Dropſie	40	Sciatica	1
Drownd two, one at St.Kath. Tower, and one at Lambeth	2	Scowring	13
		Scurvy	1
Feaver	353	Sore legge	1
Fiſtula	1	Spotted Feaver and Purples	190
Flox and Small-pox	10	Starved at Nurſe	1
Flux	2	Stilborn	8
Found dead in the Street at St.Bartholomew the Leſs	1	Stone	2
		Stopping of the ſtomach	16
Frighted	1	Strangury	1
Gangrene	1	Suddenly	1
Gowt	1	Surfeit	87
Grief	1	Teeth	113
Griping in the Guts	74	Thruſh	3

SOURCE 4 Bill of Mortality (list of deaths) for one week in London in 1665

5. What do you think 'plague water' might be?
6. What measures did Samuel Pepys take to avoid catching the plague?
7. What measures did he see or hear of other people taking?

Leather hat
Mask with glass eyes and beak stuffed with perfume or spices

Leather gloves

Stick to drive people away

Gown of waxed cloth over leather breeches

SOURCE 6 A plague doctor's uniform

---

1. On your own copy of Source 7 write notes around the outside of each picture explaining in detail what is going on in that picture. You will need to refer to the rest of the evidence on pages 83 and 84.

SOURCE 7 Three scenes from a leaflet about the Plague published in 1666

SOURCE 8 In 1665 the Lord Mayor gave these orders to all Londoners to try to stop the Plague from spreading

66
■ *Examiners: to enquire what houses be visited [by illness] and what persons be sick, and of what diseases. And if they find any person sick of the infection the house shall be shut up for a month and none can leave the house. Every house infected to be marked with a red cross a foot long with these words: 'Lord Have Mercy Upon Us.'*
■ *Searchers: Women searchers to be appointed. They shall make a search and report whether the persons do die of the infection, or of what other diseases. No searcher be permitted to keep any shop or stall, or work as a laundress.*
■ *Watchmen: For every infected house there be appointed watchmen, one for the day, and the other for the night. They have a special care that no person goes in or out of infected houses.*
■ *Householders: Every householder must keep the street before his door swept all the week long.*
■ *Rakers and dog-killers: The filth of houses be daily carried away by the rakers. No hogs, cats or conies [rabbits] to be kept in the city. Dogs to be killed by the dog-killers.*
■ *The burial of the dead must be always before sunrise or after sunset. No friend can accompany the corpse to church upon pain of having his house shut up. All the graves shall be at least six feet deep.*
99

---

2. Look at Source 8. Which of the jobs described do you think is the most dangerous?

Activity

Work in pairs. One of you is A, the other B.
A Use Sources 5–8 to make a list of the methods people used to avoid the Plague in the seventeenth century.
   Then design a poster to be put up in London in 1665 telling people how to avoid the Plague. Include all the methods in your list.
B Your teacher will tell you what actually caused the Plague. Use this information to design a poster telling people how to avoid the Plague.
   How different are the two posters?

The Great Fire of London: a blessing in disguise?

In September 1666 the Plague was still going strong. Then, early on the morning of Sunday 2 September, after a long hot summer, another disaster struck — the Great Fire of London.

London's buildings were made of wood and the houses were very close together, so fires could spread easily. But householders refused to allow their houses to be pulled down to create spaces where fires could not spread. Londoners were used to small fires breaking out. Samuel Pepys saw the fire on the night of 2 September, but simply went back to bed!

By the morning, fanned by an east wind, the fire was out of control. It spread quickly along the river-front, which was packed full of timber, pitch and oil.

Buildings were now being blown up with gunpowder to stop the fire spreading, but it was too late. The fire was unstoppable. You can see from Source 9 how much of the city it destroyed. By Tuesday 4 September it looked as if the whole city would be lost. But then the wind dropped. The firefighters could begin to douse the flames. By Friday it was all over. The damage was assessed (Source 10). Most people thought London could never be rebuilt.

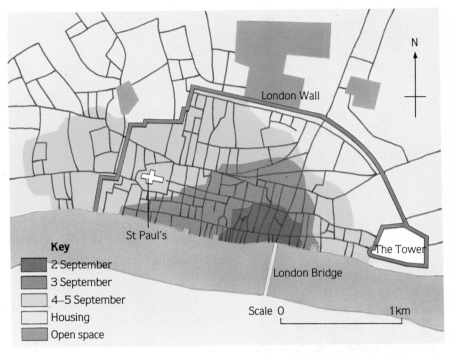

SOURCE 9 Map showing the spread of the fire

Key
- 2 September
- 3 September
- 4–5 September
- Housing
- Open space

SOURCE 10 Damage to London

" ■ *13,000 houses destroyed*
■ *87 children dead*
■ *52 company halls (the backbone of London's trade and industry) destroyed*
■ *The total loss was £10 million, at a time when London's annual income was only £12,000.* "

SOURCE 11 A painting of the Great Fire, made not long afterwards

1. On the map your teacher will give you, mark where you think the artist of Source 11 was.
2. Explain why the fire spread so quickly.

HOW DID LONDON CHANGE?

London rebuilt

Before the Great Fire London had been dirty, unhealthy and overcrowded. There was now a chance to build a new town. Rebuilding on this scale was unknown at that time, but it succeeded.

■ Over 100 streets were widened.

■ Timber was banned for building and red brick and white stone were used instead.

■ The dirty, polluted Fleet River was canalised (straightened) and eventually covered over.

■ 51 new churches were built, including a new St Paul's Cathedral – all of them designed by Sir Christopher Wren.

■ By 1671 9000 houses were complete.

By the early eighteenth century London was a cleaner and safer city. The streets and buildings looked as if they had been planned properly. For the first time rows of houses were all built in the same style and the same size. London now had some of the most elegant buildings in Europe. The rebuilding also made it more difficult for Plague to spread. After 1666 London never suffered another Plague epidemic.

London in the 1700s

In eighteenth-century London life was changing too. In the 1700s business and trade were growing in many parts of the United Kingdom. London was the financial powerhouse of this expansion. Banking and business grew quickly, with new offices being built all the time.

London was also Britain's biggest and busiest port. Flowing into and out of it each day was a rapidly expanding world trade. This was putting into the hands and mouths of people all around Britain products and foods that would have been completely unknown 250 years earlier.

> **SOURCE 13** From the journal of a seventeenth-century visitor to London
>
> 6 *Supper being finished they set on the table half a dozen pipes and a packet of tobacco.*
>
> *Smoking is the general custom for both women and men. They say it destroys the humours of the brain.* 9

1. Compare Source 12 with Source 1. Make two lists: one of features of London in 1500, the other of features of London in 1723.
2. Do you think the Great Fire of London was a blessing in disguise?

SOURCE 12 An engraving of London in 1723

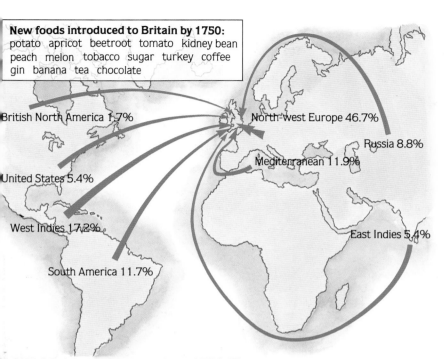

New foods introduced to Britain by 1750:
potato apricot beetroot tomato kidney bean peach melon tobacco sugar turkey coffee gin banana tea chocolate

British North America 1.7%

North-west Europe 46.7%

Russia 8.8%

Mediterranean 11.9%

United States 5.4%

West Indies 17.2%

East Indies 5.4%

South America 11.7%

SOURCE 14 London's trade in 1750. The arrows show where London's main imports came from

SOURCE 15 A coffee house

Activity

You are a visitor from Germany in London in 1750. Design a 'wish you were here' postcard to send home. On one side there should be a picture of some aspect of London. On the other side, describe some of the things you have seen in London.

SOURCE 16
The coat of arms of John Hawkins, a slave trader

London also became a centre for the infamous and cruel slave trade. Slave traders such as John Hawkins got rich by capturing people from West Africa and selling them as slaves to farmers in the Caribbean and America.

From the 1570s onwards African people were also brought as slaves to Britain – mostly to London – and slave sales such as the one in Source 17 were held at pubs in London.

Most black people in England lived in London, but by no means all were slaves. Some had a trade. Others were entertainers. Others soldiers.

SOURCE 17 From a London newspaper, 1744

"*To be sold: A pretty little negro boy, about nine years old, and well limbed. He is to be seen at the Dolphin Tavern.*"

In 1702 Fleet Street became the centre of a flourishing new industry – newspaper publishing. Now that people had time to relax and money to spend, coffee houses appeared where men would sit for hours, read the papers and discuss all the latest political developments.

A tour around Britain

IF YOU travelled around Britain in the mid-1700s what kind of country would you see? Did one part of the country differ from another? Had things changed since 1500?

In the 1720s the writer Daniel Defoe made several journeys round Britain and published his account of what he saw in a collection of letters called *A Tour Through the Whole Island of Great Britain*. We are going to follow him on his journeys.

All the written sources on the next six pages come from his book. And all the pictures are from the eighteenth century and show the things that Defoe wrote about and would have seen.

Defoe travelled at different times, by all the means of transport available – by horse, foot, river barge and, most often, stage coach. By 1750 stage coaches were making regular runs between London and the main towns shown in Source 1. In 1750 it took two and a half days to get to Birmingham and six days to get to Exeter. Horses were changed at an inn at the end of every 15km 'stage'.

SOURCE 1 Map of Britain in 1750, showing the largest towns

▶ **SOURCE 2** A stage coach changing horses at an inn-yard

Journey 1: East Anglia

One good place to start your journey is in London. Travelling north takes you through the marshes of Essex.

SOURCE 3 From Defoe's *Tour*: the coastal area of Dagenham

66 *These lowlands are held by farmers, cow-keepers and grazing butchers who live in or near London. They buy large fat sheep in Smithfield market in September and keep them here till Christmas, when they sell them at a good price.* 99

SOURCE 4 Suffolk and Norfolk

66 *Here [Southwold] cattle are fattened with turnips. Suffolk is also famous for furnishing London with turkeys. More are bred here than in the rest of England. The geese and turkeys travel to London on foot.*

When we come into Norfolk we see vast manufacture carried on by the Norwich weavers, who employ all the country round in spinning yarn for them. In and around Norwich 120,000 people are employed in woollen and silk manufacture. 99

▲ **SOURCE 5** Engraving of Norwich, 1724

SOURCE 6 The land around Ipswich

The country here is applied chiefly to corn, most of which is shipped off for London. Sometimes they load corn here for Holland. 🙟

1. What different activities are mentioned in Sources 3, 4 and 6?
2. What evidence is there that this part of the country was important for supplying London?

Journey 2: the South West

SOURCE 7 Drawing of Dorchester in 1750. Defoe commented: 'The Downs around Dorchester are exceedingly pleasant. There are 600,000 sheep fed on the Downs within six miles of the town. Farmers come to Burford Fair to buy them and take them back to Kent, Surrey and Oxfordshire'

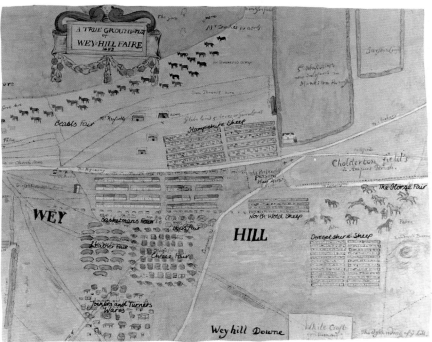

SOURCE 8 Wey Hill Fair – a plan drawn in 1683. When Defoe visited Wey Hill Fair in the 1720s it was 'the greatest sheep fair this nation can show'

◀ **SOURCE 9** A Cornish tin mine drawn in the 1770s. As Defoe travelled into Cornwall, between Launceston and Liskeard, he found many tin mines with 'some of the richest veins of metal in the whole country'

1. People came from all over central and southern England to Wey Hill Fair. Design a poster advertising the fair. Tell people about all the things they can buy there.

A TOUR AROUND BRITAIN

Journey 3: the West and Wales

SOURCE 10 Bristol, painted in the 1720s. Defoe was impressed: 'The merchants of this city have the greatest trade other than London. The shopkeepers maintain carriers with all the main towns from Southampton to Nottingham'

> **1.** What activities can you see going on in Source 10?

> **2.** What industries can you see going on in Source 11?

▼ SOURCE 11 The different industries to be found on the Welsh coast in 1748

SOURCE 12 Harvest time at Bixton in Gloucestershire, painted in the 1730s

3. What impression of the countryside do you get from the painting in Source 12?

SOURCE 13 A carrier waggon, painted in 1695. These travelled regularly on popular trade routes between towns

Journey 4: the North

SOURCE 14 Map of Leeds in 1725. Defoe described the cloth market that took place in the main street twice a week: 'You see ten and twenty thousand pounds of cloth, sometimes more, bought and sold in little more than an hour . . . for use at home . . . to send to London . . . or for overseas buyers from Holland and Germany'

1. Look at Source 14. Can you find the site of the cloth market?
2. Work out from the map what other trades were carried out in Leeds.
3. How many places of worship (churches or meeting houses) can you find? Are they all Church of England?

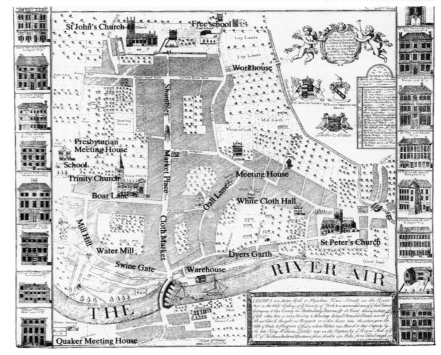

SOURCE 15 In Derby Defoe saw 'the only silk mill in the country. It is turned by water and performs the labour of many hands.' Historians now believe this was probably the first factory in England. This drawing, made in 1747, shows the factory's machines for winding and twisting silk

SOURCE 16 Derbyshire's lead miners

"*The man was clothed all in leather. He had a leather cap without brims. We could not understand anything the man said. He was as pale as a dead corpse. Besides his basket of tools, he brought up with him [about 38kg] of ore. This made him come heaving and struggling up. He was working at 60 fathoms [360 feet] deep. His wife and five children lived in a cave in the mountain. She washed the ore for 3d a day. But everything was clean and tidy and there was a side of bacon hanging. The children looked plump and fat and clean. Before we left we made up a little lump of money. As I pressed it into the woman's hand she dissolved into tears. She told me she had not seen so much money for many months.*"

1. Do you think the family in Source 16 was poor?
2. Do you think the woman's husband would look anything like the lead miner in Source 17?

SOURCE 17 Painting of a Pennine leadminer, 1760

Journey 5: the Highlands and Islands

SOURCE 18 Wives carry their husbands out to their fishing boats at Inverness, 1725

SOURCE 19 Perth

"*The chief business of the town is linen manufacture. The River Tay is navigable up to the town and they ship off a great quantity of linen, all for England.*"

SOURCE 20 Lithgow

"*The water of the loch here is said to be the best in Scotland for whitening the linen cloth. So a great deal of linen made in other parts of the country is brought here to be whitened.*"

SOURCE 21 House on the island of Islay, 1772

1. Write a detailed description of the house in Source 21. Include the number of children and animals, what people are doing, and how it is furnished.

SOURCE 22 Stages of linen manufacture, drawn in the 1780s

A

B

C

D

E

2. Match the captions in the box to the correct pictures in Source 22.
3. Which of the jobs were done in people's homes?

Back home again

1. On your own map of Britain, mark and name the places mentioned on the five journeys. You will need to consult an atlas.
2. By each place mark the activities mentioned by Defoe.
3. Mark in all the trade routes that Defoe mentions.
4. Now make a list of all the different jobs mentioned which people did at that time.
5. Find three differences and three similarities between the north of the country and the south.
6. Choose three pictures that show the different lives that women led in different parts of the country. Describe in detail what the women are doing.
7. Are there any aspects of life seen by Defoe that you think had not changed much since 1500? Are there any which had changed a good deal?
8. What do you think? Was Britain in the 1720s a modern country?

Captions

- Beating the flax to separate the fibres, and 'hackling' them to make them lie in a single direction
- Boiling, spinning and reeling the yarn
- Winding the yarn and weaving it into cloth
- A bleach mill – boiling, wringing and treating the cloth
- Measuring the cloth and making it into rolls

Activity

It is 1750. Where in Britain would you least like to live? Where would you *most* like to live? Design an advertisement attracting people to move there.

Glossary

absolute monarch   a monarch who is not bound by the rules of a **constitution**, so has complete power

constitution   document laying down rules within which a monarch and government must operate. A constitutional monarch is one who has to obey the rules of the constitution, so does not have complete power

Feudal System   traditional system in England, where a peasant held land in return for services and taxes paid to the landowner

gentry   class of rich landowners just below the nobility in social position

heretic   person whose religious beliefs are against the main teachings of the Christian Church

Jacobite   supporter of James Stuart and his son 'Bonnie Prince Charlie' in their claim to the British throne in the eighteenth century

Justice of the Peace (JP)   an official appointed by the government to keep law and order and try minor court cases in a town or county

monastery   home of a community of monks

Parliamentarian   suporter of Parliament during the English Civil War

propaganda   limited, often biased, information which is spread about to persuade people to support certain beliefs or government policies, for example

Puritan   strict Protestant who wanted to simplify forms of worship, keep Sunday holy, etc.

referendum   a way of deciding a political question by getting all voters to vote for or against it

Republic   form of government without a monarchy

Royalist   supporter of the King during the English Civil War

Stuarts   royal family of Britain from James I to Queen Anne (1603–1714)

Tudors   royal family of England and Wales from Henry VII to Elizabeth (1485–1603)

Index

Discovering the Past in Key Stage 3

Y7	■ *Contrasts and Connections*	Pupils' Book	0 7195 4938 8
		Teachers' Resource Book	0 7195 4962 0
	■ *Discovering The Roman Empire*	Pupils' Book	0 7195 5179 X
		Teachers' Evaluation Pack	0 7195 5180 3
	■ *Discovering Medieval Realms*	Pupils' Book	0 7195 5177 3
		Teachers' Evaluation Pack	0 7195 5178 1
	■ *Medieval Realms Special Needs Support Materials*	Picture Pack	0 7195 5382 2
		Teachers' Resource Book	0 7195 5381 4
	■ *Castles and Cathedrals*	Pupils' Book	0 7195 4952 3
		Teachers' Evaluation Pack	0 7195 4979 5
Y8	■ *Societies in Change*	Pupils' Book	0 7195 4975 2
		Teachers' Resource Book	0 7195 4976 0
	■ *Discovering The Making of the UK*	Pupils' Book	0 7195 7052 2
		Teachers' Evaluation Pack	0 7195 7053 0
	■ *The Making of the UK Special Needs Support Materials*	Picture Pack	0 7195 7044 1
		Teachers' Resource Book	0 7195 7043 3
	■ *The Renaissance*	Pupils' Book	0 7195 5186 2
		Teachers' Resource Book	0 7195 5187 0
Y9	■ *Peace and War*	Pupils' Book	0 7195 4977 9
		Teachers' Resource Book	0 7195 4978 7
	■ *Expansion, Trade and Industry/Britain 1750–1900 Special Needs Support Materials*	Picture Pack	0 7195 7046 8
		Teachers' Resource Book	0 7195 7045 X
	■ *Britain and the Great War*	Pupils' Book	0 7195 5148 X
		Teachers' Resource Book	0 7195 5152 8
	■ *The Changing Role of Women*	Pupils' Book	0 7195 5106 4
		Teachers' Evaluation Pack	0 7195 5107 2

Available from John Murray, 50 Albemarle Street, London W1X 4BD